Today a Flying Bear Will Kill Me

Quests, Inquiries, and Misadventures

E. J. Myers

Today a Flying Bear Will Kill Me

Quests, Inquiries, and Misadventures

E. J. Myers

Montemayor Press

Montpelier, Vermont

"Boxtop Satori" first appeared in *College Hill Review* (Summer, 2014); "Camera Obscura" in *Wilderness House Literary Review* (Spring, 2019); and "Provincial Gods" in *The Nasiona* (April, 2019).

To these brothers
with deep gratitude
for their wisdom and friendship:

Steve Fedder

Burt Kimmelman

Andy Sweet

Today a Flying Bear Will Kill Me

Quests, Inquiries, and Misadventures

E. J. Myers

Contents

How will you go about finding that thing the nature of which is totally unknown to you?

—Meno, quoted in Plato, "Meno"

The soul wanted what it wanted. It had its own natural language. It sat unhappily on super-structures of explanation, poor bird, not knowing which way to fly.

—Saul Bellow, *Mr. Sammler's Planet*

I never was lost in the woods in my whole life, though once I was confused for three days.

—Daniel Boone

Forethoughts

Today a Flying Bear Will Kill Me

They never saw it coming. Nobody could have seen it coming. Nobody would have woken in the morning and thought, "Today a flying bear will kill me." Even when it happened, the Canadians couldn't have grasped the sight of a flying bear materializing out of nowhere and arriving to kill them. Yet a flying bear materialized out of nowhere and killed them. As one of many news reports described this event:

> A "flying bear" killed two Canadians instantly when a freak car accident propelled the black bear through the front windshield of a second vehicle.
>
> A car slammed into the black bear at night on a rural Quebec highway about 25 miles north of Ottawa, the Canadian capital, local police told the Canadian Broadcasting Corporation.
>
> The 440-pound bear was thrown into the air and hit an SUV traveling in the opposite direction, smashing through the SUV's front windshield and then out the back window.
>
> The driver of the SUV, a 25-year-old Ottawa woman, was pronounced dead at the scene, as was a 40-year-old passenger sitting behind her. But the driver's boyfriend, sitting in the front passenger seat, escaped with only minor injuries.
>
> The two occupants of the first car that hit the bear were not hurt.
>
> The bear was killed on impact.[1]

What difference does it make whether the Angel of Death is a flying bear or a less exotic assassin among the host of lethal seraphim—a falling tree, a car crossing the median, a pill lodged in the windpipe, a clot stuck in the cardiac arteries? No matter what the means of ending your life, you're dead. All deaths create the same result. All deaths take human beings' accomplishments—deeds done, love given, wisdom gained, insights reached—and sweep them away. All deaths are in this sense absurd.

SOME YEARS AGO, while taking stock of my life in the ordinary way that many people do during late middle age, I compiled a list of my own near-death experiences. The list documented fifteen incidents in which I came unmistakably close to dying. A friend commented later, when I mentioned the list, "That's so *morbid!*" I didn't perceive my compilation as morbid. I considered it an exercise in perspective. The effort led not to dread or depression but to what I call a hallelujah moment. I found myself astonished and delighted *to be alive at all*. The list provided an account of identifiable incidents in which my time on earth could have ended abruptly—but hadn't. All the better, then, to feel gratitude, delight, even jubilation.

The incidents started early: an incident of near-drowning in a hotel swimming pool when I was seven. Family travels during my boyhood and teen years included several near-catastrophes involving planes, buses, and cars, mostly in Latin America. At age twelve, I survived—along with everyone else on the planet—when the Cuban Missile Crisis ended in a stalemate rather than in a nuclear conflagration. (Historians have clarified since then that World War III failed to occur in October of 1962 partly because a sole Russian submarine captain countermanded an order to fire nuclear torpedoes at American ships during the U.S. naval blockade of Cuba.) Later near-misses occurred mostly during mountaineering trips in Colorado, Mexico, and Peru: near-falls, near-avalanches, and near-lightning strikes. Most potentially lethal events, however, especially during my thirties and later, resulted from ordinary close calls in planes and cars. It's true, of course, that many other brushes with death may have occurred, or nearly occurred, without my awareness. None of us necessarily knows which car rides almost led to an accident but somehow didn't. We never know which airline flights included a serious in-flight problem that the pilots somehow avoided or resolved. We never learn which lightning bolts could have struck us while we hiked but discharged somewhere else. Like death itself, the absence of death is often a mystery.

The patterns throughout my life were clear: cars, airplanes, and mountains have presented the greatest risks. Avoiding mountains, or at least deciding not to climb them, eliminated the dangers I faced earlier. Avoiding cars and planes has been far more difficult. Short of joining the Amish, there's no easy way around modern transportation and its risks. (Even the Amish sometimes die in road accidents.)

FOR SEVERAL WEEKS during March of 1983, my wife and I traveled in Mexico—first in the Yucatán, later in the state of Oaxaca. Edith then flew back to New York, where we were living, late that month. I took a bus from Mexico City to the state of Guanajuato to visit some Mexican friends; then I returned by bus to the capital. On the morning of April fourth, I went to the airport in order to catch an Aeroméxico flight to JFK.

Right off I learned of a problem. "I'm at the Mexico City airport starting what looks like a long wait," I noted in a journal entry written at the time. "The inevitable wait," I added. "This airline isn't called 'AeroMaybe' for nuthin'. I'll be surprised if we leave before noon." The wait dragged on for twelve hours. Aeroméxico staffers came out periodically, made confusing announcements to the passengers, contradicted themselves repeatedly, and with each clarification left us more befuddled than before. One gate agent stated (in English), "The plane, it has a small fault." The words I heard him say later, in Spanish, were *falla mecánica*—a mechanical failure. Clearly a significant problem. I've always felt that whenever pre-flight safety is an issue, the airline should take any time necessary to solve the problem. Many of my fellow passengers, most of them Americans, disagreed. They just wanted to leave as soon as possible. "The worst of the complainers are the hot-under-the-collar New Yorkers," I noted in my journal. "There's been much ranting and raving, bickering, and insulting of the personnel. The passengers, especially the Americans, are fit to kill." I felt disheartened and frustrated but unsure what to do. Should I try to book another flight? Should I just muddle through and wait? Most of a day passed before the gate agents allowed us to board a plane. Then, deluded into thinking that our ordeal had ended, we sat on the tarmac for yet another hour. Neither the captain nor anyone else clarified the situation.

When we took off at long last, I thought my problems were over. They almost were, though not in the way I'd anticipated, and with a potential finality that I couldn't possibly have wanted. The jet, an old Boeing 707, rolled down the runway. And rolled. And rolled. Mexico City sits in a valley floor at 7,500 feet in altitude. Airliners take a long time gaining sufficient lift in the thin air; hence they need a long roll before takeoff. Our time on the runway went on and on—first in a way that seemed appropriate for the setting, then in a way that began to concern me. It kept going. Surely the pilot would abort the takeoff... He didn't. At long last I felt the plane tilt gently upward. I saw the tarmac start to drop away. A little. Very little. At once I saw tile and concrete roofs, rooftop water tanks, telephone and power lines, multicolored walls of buildings, streets, cars, trucks . . . Our plane was airborne, but only by a hundred feet. We stayed aloft. We didn't rise. We didn't fall. Looking out my window, I could see not only cars and buildings but individual people going about their tasks in one of the less-affluent *barrios* north of the airport. People walked down a street. Women hung laundry on clotheslines. Children played in a schoolyard. Why weren't we gaining altitude? Why was the plane flying so slowly? The passenger next to me, a middle-aged Mexican woman, gazed past me and out the window. Around us I heard no commotion, no cries of anguish or fear. All of us on the plane must have felt more baffled than afraid. Because no dramatic incident had occurred—no collision with another aircraft, no explosion of an engine—we could persuade ourselves that nothing was amiss. Yet a deep ache started gnawing at my gut. The Valley of Mexico is huge, but at some point a plane must gain sufficient altitude to clear the mountains ringing the valley floor. Some of the peaks, such as the famous volcanoes Popocatepetl and Ixtaccihuatl, are over 16,000 feet in height. Others are eight or ten thousand feet high. A plane flying a hundred feet off the ground doesn't need much of a hill to terminate its journey. At what point would our lollygagging rattletrap plane simply run out of room and smash into a mountainside?

By now I felt intense alarm. I couldn't believe that we wouldn't crash. Paralyzed, I started to do what many people do under the circumstances—not reviewing my life, though maybe that would come next, but worrying about other issues. Edith would already be concerned about me. In 1983 the Web was still eight years in the future. Even placing a long-distance call from the airport to New York would have been difficult, and I hadn't done it. Perhaps she had phoned Manhattan's Aeroméxico office for an update. If my plane crashed, as now seemed inevitable, Edith would learn of the accident on the news. I felt a deep anxiety about the hardships she would endure in the aftermath. I felt a stiletto stab of anguish that I would never see her again.

Another thought crossed my mind. Mexico City, densely populated, isn't a great place to crash-land an airliner. I found it hard to believe that scores of people, even hundreds, wouldn't be killed if Flight 243 plowed into one of the *barrios*. Here again I realized that nothing I could do might alter the situation.

The plan would smash into a working-class neighborhood, explode, strew aircraft parts over a couple of city blocks, engulf the area in flaming jet fuel, and slaughter the residents trapped there.

Then, for reasons that weren't clear at the time and that will stay unknown forever, the plane started to rise. I say rise rather than climb because I perceived no upward pitch. I simply saw the ground below us, the buildings and the streets and the billboards, growing smaller. This, despite what must have been the gradual incline as we approached the hills and mountains north of the valley. The rising continued. The flight continued. To my astonishment and jubilation, we didn't crash. Our plane simply flew onward. We angled northeast across the Mexican states of Hidalgo and Veracruz. We crossed the Gulf of Mexico, we angled across the American South, we proceeded to a routine landing at JFK. When we touched down, all the passengers erupted into applause.

I've pondered over the years since then how for several minutes after takeoff, I was the flying bear. Or, at a minimum, I was one of a hundred twenty mini-bears inside the belly of a mega-bear. The people on the ground never saw us coming. Nobody could have seen us coming. Nobody expected a plane to materialize out of nowhere and arrive to kill them. Yet our plane appeared out of nowhere and arrived to kill them.

And then we didn't. We gained altitude, headed north, and flew away.

Provincial Gods

Once, long ago, I came face to face with a deity, an earthy god in Peru, and the meeting did not go well. More accurately, I crossed paths with an ancient god's effigy deep inside a buried temple. *It is a fearful thing to fall into the hands of the living God,* wrote St. Paul. Maybe so, but I have to take the apostle's word for it. My own experience—ending up nose to nose with a dead god—was no picnic, either.

This encounter took place in the ruins of Chavín de Huántar, a ceremonial center that one of South America's oldest, most influential pre-Columbian cultures built in fifteen stages between 1200 BCE and 800 CE. (The Inca empire, by contrast, flourished much more recently—between 1425 CE and 1532 CE.) Abandoned for over a millennium, the Chavín culture's religious center lay in ruins and received few visitors until the mid-twentieth century.[1]

A longtime friend had joined me in 1977 for a trek to Chavín. Scott Thomas and I, having met in junior high school, had hiked and camped together, mostly in the Colorado Rockies, over a period of many years. During the mid-Seventies, we had speculated about traveling to Peru. Now our trekking junket had begun. We flew to Lima and traveled overland to Huaraz, a small city in the north-central Peruvian Andes that would serve as our urban base camp for trips into the mountains. At some point, however, Scott informed me that a college friend of his, Peter, would be joining us. I hesitated to object despite feeling concerned about the changes in our collaboration. Peter arrived, settled in with us, and then, a day before our planned departure, announced that two of his own friends, Jane and Dave, would be coming along as well. To complicate matters further, Scott suddenly fell ill with a severe intestinal virus and felt too sick to make the trip. With Scott sidelined, I abruptly found myself heading into the hinterlands with people I didn't even know.

I felt uneasy around Peter from the start. Talkative, funny, and clearly bright, he seemed an affable con man. He was good-natured as he manipulated people around him but manipulative all the same. His frequent comments about drug deals alarmed me. "Scoring coke here is like buying sugar," he announced. I asked if he worried about getting busted. "Busted?" he exclaimed with a laugh. "Hell, no! Even if you get caught, possession is a bribable offense." When I expressed concern about my possible guilt by association, Peter brushed off my worries. I felt angry and appalled that he would disregard my feelings on an issue that could land us all in jail. "It's nothing to get so uptight about," he noted, adding with a laugh: "If you think I'm bad company, you don't really have to join the trek, do you?" I could have pointed out that he was actually joining *my* trek, but I decided to hold off. Peter dismissed the point. "Let's just go there, okay?" he said. "There's safety in numbers."

Jane and Dave? A twenty-something couple from California, they seemed cordial enough and at least showed no interest in drug deals. On the other hand, they manifested some attitudes I've found common and troubling in people who have visited so many places—in their case, dozens of countries over a period of several years—that they've become jaded. Nothing inspired their curiosity. New places seemed important chiefly as names to cross off a list. Landscapes, people, history, languages, art, cuisine, customs: everything struck them as irrelevant, problematic, or uninteresting. These attitudes held true regarding north-central Peru. Worse yet, they expressed criticism and even contempt for almost every aspect of what they encountered. Peruvian food was bad, the hotels uncomfortable, the locals annoying, the language confusing, the customs a nuisance. "Peru is supposed to be such a cool country," Dave commented during an early conversation.

"Frankly, I think it's overrated." I had joined forces with fellow travelers who regarded our venture as a waste of time from the outset.

On June 30th, the four of us hitched up the main valley to a town called Olleros, then hiked several miles on a steep dirt road heading due east. Most of this region, the Callejón de Huaylas, is spectacular—a hundred-mile-long valley flanked by two Andean *cordilleras,* one of them the world's highest equatorial mountain range, its summits reaching over 22,000 feet in altitude—but our route was less remarkable than other places I'd seen in the area. Yellow-brown grasslands rolled away in all directions without offering any views of the glaciated peaks. This was the *puna,* high tundra covered with tan, tufty *ichu* grass. The hiking offered a sense of relief, however, after many days of inactivity in Huaraz. Even so, I felt uneasy to be undertaking a major trek with these disagreeable companions. Would they be competent hikers? Could I trust them in an emergency? Would we get along?

AFTER THAT DAY'S FIRST WALK, we camped at around 14,000 feet. The site was typical of the *puna.* I saw no signs of people or livestock. I was already accustomed to backpacking in the Andes—I had trekked for several weeks during a trip in 1971— so I knew that our surroundings weren't unusual. I also knew that despite the barren landscape, this place was probably inhabited. What foreigners often perceive as exotic wilderness in Peru is what the *campesinos,* the indigenous residents of these areas, would regard as just an ordinary rural setting. I knew we had probably pitched our camp on someone's grazing land. Was this land held in common by local villagers? Or did it belong to a specific family? Either way, we were trespassing. Local customs generally allowed respectful parties to cross the land, even to camp there briefly. I felt neither surprised nor alarmed when a middle-aged man stopped by that evening to visit us and, I assumed, to assess our intentions.

Like many male Andean *mestizos*—men of mixed Spanish-Indigenous heritage—he wore clothing that to an American, at least, looked incongruous: homespun woolen pants, tattered V-neck sweater, baggy woolen sports jacket, and misshapen fedora. (Men of fully Indigenous background probably would have been attired in tire-soled sandals, knee pants, homespun cotton shirt, and woolen poncho.) This man, fortyish in age, looked as if he might have wandered away from a business meeting years ago somewhere in a coastal Peruvian city but had never changed his outfit. He appeared at once dapper and bedraggled.

"*¿De dunde vienen ustedes, gringu?*" he asked me in Quechua-accented Spanish—Where are you from, Foreigner?

"Colorado," I told him, avoiding mention of the United States.

He nodded gravely. "*¿Es parte de lus Estadus Unidus?*"

"It is," I admitted, then changed the subject: "We're hiking to Chavín so we can see the ruins."

Another nod. *Campesinos* I had spoken with in the past often expressed amazement that foreigners would choose to walk long distances when they could have ridden. Why, too, would anyone travel so far just to see mountains and ruins? He probably couldn't comprehend why we gringos would expend so much effort and expense to visit such a remote place. In any case, I wanted to reassure this man that we wouldn't linger. Outsiders often inspire anxiety among the Indigenous population—an attitude that's neither surprising nor unjustified, since Europeans and Americans have caused them so much damage and grief ever since the Spanish *conquistadores* first showed up in 1535.

"May we camp on your land for one night?" I asked.

"*Sí, está bien.*" I detected neither hospitality nor enthusiasm in his words, only cautious consent.

We continued chatting. I wanted to put this man more at ease, to show him that we presented no threat to him or his family.

We were just four gringos passing through. We discussed the land, the weather, and the reasons why foreigners visit Peru to hike and climb mountains. I don't remember how or when, but somehow the discussion turns to *pishtacos*. I had heard about these mythical figures as a teenager—also known as *pishtacus* or *pistacus*—back when my family lived in Lima for two years during the 1960's. According to Andean folk mythology, *pishtacos* are henchmen of the devil who appear unexpectedly to perpetrate sinful deeds—kidnapping children, murdering adults, even cooking them to render their body fat. These evil creatures often resemble American and European males: tall, bearded, boot-wearing men. Hearing mention of *pishtacos* while talking with this landowner—I myself being bearded and booted, though tall relative only to the often short *campesinos*— made me nervous.[2] At some point, speaking calmly, he said, *"Quizás tú eres un pishtaco."* Maybe *you* are a henchman of the devil. This oblique accusation alarmed me. What would this man's speculation mean about his attitude toward us—or about his possible actions while we trespassed on his land? If he believed we were henchmen of the devil, what might he do to us? During my family's mid-1960's stay in Peru, a Peace Corps volunteer had told my parents that an American he knew, a young priest living in the same Andean village, had been accosted one night and killed, his throat slit, because of rumors that he was a *pishtaco*.

The *campesino* and I chatted for a while longer. Peter, Dave, and Jane, who spoke almost no Spanish and showed neither interest in nor respect for our host as I talked with him, didn't join the conversation. All three of them acted rather miffed that anyone would bother us while we fixed our supper. Then, after I assured the landowner once again that we would leave in the morning, he turned and walked off.

WE PASSED THE NIGHT without incident. The dreadful fantasy I envisioned on going to sleep—that the *campesino* would come back and nip our deviltry in the bud—never came to pass. My companions and I woke at dawn, ate breakfast, folded our tents, and packed our gear. We then set off and continued hiking up the valley. Once again the scenery was unremarkable, just a scattering of peaks with small glaciers descending from their slopes, drab *puna*. The hiking wasn't hard, but the effort felt tedious. The wind slapped us. The scenery offered no solace or inspiration. Even so, I felt eager when I grasped that we would reach Chavín within five or six hours. Having broken camp at nine, we cleared the pass by eleven. A downhill path now lay before us. Yet the hiking grew more difficult despite our now having gravity to our advantage: descents can be strenuous. We were passing through the Quebrada Huachecsa, one of the steepest gorges in this section of the Andes. The trail was wide but uneven and rocky. Even a minor slip could have caused a major accident. The final stretch angled us down a massive trench whose granite walls rose almost vertically on our right and our left. Then, as we neared Chavín, I saw the drab little village and, off to the right, the excavated ruins. The site looked much more extensive than I'd anticipated.

Walking into town, I felt relieved to have finished our trek. Jane, David, and Peter had been able hikers. We explored the town center—low, whitewashed, tile-roofed houses clustered around a dusty Plaza de Armas—and we managed to find acceptable lodging. Like many such hotels in backwoods Peru, this one consisted of four one-story structures forming a square-sided O and facing a central courtyard. The buildings' adobe walls were crudely plastered and whitewashed both inside and out. The rooms were monastic: two beds, a rough-hewn table, a chair, and a single window looking out onto the courtyard. Each bed consisted of a sagging straw mattress, threadbare sheets, a single blanket, and a pillow. I had grown accustomed to such hotels throughout my travels in Peru; I almost enjoyed their austerity. This one would serve our purposes, especially since there would be nothing better in a little town like Chavín.

Peter and I would share one room; Dave and Jane would take another. In the courtyard, rabbits hopped about while some children chased one another, shouting and laughing. In short, the place was a provincial Third World inn much like those I'd come to know well during my earlier travels.

We settled in. We all felt so tired that we didn't venture out that afternoon. We napped, then walked to the Plaza de Armas, sat there for a while, returned to the hotel, and read our books. That evening, the four of us ate dinner at a scruffy little restaurant. Both before and after the meal, we drank beer at a different café. The town was quiet and dark. I was exhausted.

DURING THE 1970's, Chavín was a well-known but rarely visited archaeological site. The town and the site received little attention compared to, say, Machu Picchu, located almost four hundred miles to the south; few foreigners in Peru, most of whom zeroed in on the famous "Lost City of the Incas," ever trekked to the much older site where I now found myself. Located at an altitude of 10,500 feet a hundred fifty miles north-northeast of Lima, Chavín is the remnant of a civilization that draws far less attention than the Incas' iconic ruins. Western visitors had "discovered" the site during the late nineteenth century, but indigenous residents of the area had surely known about the ceremonial center from time immemorial. Little information about the site's origins and purpose became available until the 1990's. Although early twentieth-century archaeologists grasped that the Chavín culture predated the Incas by many centuries, they significantly underestimated its age. Initial guesses dated construction at between 800 CE and 1200 CE. During the mid- and late 1990's, however, John W. Rick, a Stanford University anthropologist, used radiocarbon dating to determine that the Chavín culture actually *finished* building its city by 800CE. These estimates of the culture's development make the site many centuries older than Machu Picchu, which the Incas constructed during the 1400s. For this and other reasons, some archaeologists compare Chavín to the Sumerian ruins in Mesopotamia, both because of their age and because of the past inhabitants' profound influence on later civilizations. My longstanding interest in pre-Columbian cultures had prompted me to visit Chavín.

I AWOKE IN PAIN. My knees ached, felt warm to the touch, and were visibly swollen. The discomfort and swelling baffled me. Eighteen months later, after experiencing multiple episodes of similar symptoms, I would receive a diagnosis of sero-negative polyarthritis, a poorly understood form of joint disease, but in July of 1977 I didn't know what was happening. All I knew was that my knees had puffed up so much that I could scarcely walk. I guessed that the swelling resulted partly from my descent on the long, steep trail down through the Quebrada Huachecsa while carrying a forty-pound pack, but I had no idea how to remedy the swelling. I took two Tylenol and hoped the discomfort would ease. I joined my companions at a little café near the Plaza de Armas, where the teenage waiter served us the only available breakfast: reconstituted milk and stale bread. The four of us talked for a while, reviving, then set out for the ruins.

Walking toward the site, I couldn't see much of it as we left town. Soon, however, a grassy plaza came into view. I also saw several huge mounds flanking the site's entrance—temples? pyramids?—along with a series of dilapidated walls and the remnants of a staircase slanting against a two- or three-story story structure. Compared to other Mesoamerican and South American sites I've visited—Machu Picchu and Chan Chan in Peru, Uxmal and Chichén Itzá in Mexico—Chavín had a veiled, perplexing appearance. Only decades later would archaeologists fully excavate the ruins that in 1977 remained a dirt- and grass-covered state; and only then would they begin to understand the site's full extent and its likely purpose. I had read, however, that the ruins' still-buried condition wouldn't be an obstacle to glimpsing what's most important about Chavín. The secrets there don't lie on the surface but in an underground maze of tunnels and chambers.

The four of us wandered for a while among the ruins to view the dilapidated temples and plazas. The religious center lay at the base of a tall, broad hill—what would have been a mountain in most parts of the world didn't count for much in the Andes. Grass covered the plazas and the horizontal surfaces of many terraces. Staircases rose from the plazas to the temples. Many of the stone walls, though less tightly constructed than the Incas' much later masonry, struck me nonetheless as impressive. Peter, Jane, Dave, and I explored these areas for twenty minutes.

Then, locating the entrance to the Old Temple, we entered a dark passageway. We had brought only two flashlights to shine a path for all four of us. One of the lights was mine, fortunately, and I insisted on keeping it in my possession. Dave held the other. These two scant beams provided only enough light to make our way in. We groped our way forward with just the barest sense of what lay around us. The subterranean passageway smelled like a cave. I felt we were creating more darkness than we managed to dispel. Worse yet, we saw other hallways branching off from the one we had entered. We had entered a labyrinth. What if we got lost underground? What if the flashlights failed? At some point we heard footsteps behind us: not a welcome sound. Turning, we saw a pall of yellow light approaching. *"¿Necesitan ayuda?"* asked a low voice. Do you need help? Although initially uneasy to have a stranger join us in this claustrophobic place, I soon felt relieved that the ruin's caretaker—a dark-skinned, middle-aged man wearing rough woolen trousers, a sienna-colored poncho, and a rumpled fedora—had followed us in. Holding a kerosene lantern, he offered his assistance.

We proceeded down the hallway. With the path now more amply illuminated, we could see far more of our surroundings.

Even the lantern couldn't push away the darkness farther than twenty feet ahead, however, and the stones protruding from the walls on our left and right cast shadows ahead of us. The caretaker made a few comments about the site, his Quechua accent so thick that even I, fluent in Spanish, couldn't follow his narration. Soon we continued in silence.

Then, almost without warning, we reached the *lanzón*—Chavín's Holy of Holies. Four and a half meters tall, this effigy stands in its own chamber at the intersection of two corridors. The caretaker held up his lantern up for us to see the massive carved pillar. A jaguar face leered at us from atop a human body. A mane of snakes sprouted from the head. Fangs protruded from the mouth. Eyes peered at us from all over. The yellow lantern light, shifting, made these features move as if alive. I felt the creature's crude, bloody holiness. Gazing at this idol, I responded in ways I never had before in such a place: I felt sick to my stomach, I broke into a cold sweat, I felt faint. I was afraid in ways I couldn't explain or control. I worried about passing out. Then the reaction diminished. I kept looking, still uneasy but feeling a less visceral response. I listened to my companions make their dismissive comments. Dave said, "Well, whatever floats your boat." Peter said, "Wonder what kind of drug the sculptor-dude was taking." Then we turned, followed the caretaker back through the labyrinth, and emerged into the sunshine.

OUR VISIT TO THE RUINS continued for a while longer, then spun itself out. Peter, Jane, and Dave traded complaints about how disappointing they found Chavín—"Not a tenth as good as Machu Picchu," Dave noted. Feeling restless and exhausted, I kept to myself, said nothing, and brooded about my own experience inside the ruins. The others wanted to keep wandering, however, so I followed them briefly, then retreated to the town center once their interest in the site guttered out. I returned to the hotel. Achy and tired, I slept for a while. Ignoring the others when they showed up again, I ate bread and peanut butter in my room rather than joining everyone else at a local restaurant. I kept to myself through the afternoon: sat in the courtyard and read. Although I wanted a break from my companions, I also needed time and solitude to ponder the day. What had I experienced deep inside the ruins? Why had the stela unnerved me? What was the significance of the revulsion I felt toward its primal features?

Nothing came of my brooding, but a sense of unease lingered.

Later, the four of us joined up again to find some dinner. We circled the town square and stopped at each of the several restaurants to ask what they might be serving. Typical of provincial joints in the Andes, each place posted a small black slate listing the day's menu in chalk letters. *Lomo saltado, pescado frito, cuy al horno . . .* All four of us had traveled long enough in Peru to know that these offerings were theoretical, not actual. When we asked one of the restaurant's waiters about, say, *lomo saltado,* he replied, *"Se acabó"*—It ran out. How about the *pescado frito? "No hay"*—There isn't any. What about the *cuy al horno? "Todavía no"*—Not yet. This litany of requests and negations prompted Peter to exclaim, "These people are so damn negative! Their five national mottos are *No hay, Todavía no, No se puede, Se acabó,* and *Está prohibido.* No wonder they never get anything done!" I commented that it must be hard to live in a place where scarcity was the norm, not an aberration. "Given their negativity," Jane responded, "it's no wonder everything's so scarce."

Eventually we settled on the Restaurant Santa Rosa, right off the plaza. It was so dark and dingy, just a few tables in a single room full of smoke from a wood-fired stove, that we questioned the wisdom of eating there at all. Seeing no better alternative, however, we went ahead. The meal: fried eggs with fried potatoes. We ate in near-silence. I felt relieved to have a break from my companions' complaints. There were some distractions as well. Three drunk teenage *campesinos* sat at a nearby table, one of them singing pentatonic songs in Quechua to his pals. At some point a little boy and a pubescent girl emerged from the kitchen, seated themselves at our table, and proceeded to do their homework while we ate. I enjoyed having them present—they were much more congenial company than my fellow travelers. "What is nine times six?" the little boy asked me in Spanish. The girl showed me her grammar lesson. Jane, Dave, and Peter grumbled about these kids disrupting our meal. I ignored the gringos and chatted with the children. Nearby, a fedora-hatted woman in a dirty white cotton blouse and long woolen skirts ate soup beside a flaring stove in the otherwise dark kitchen. Several cats and dogs roamed around us, begging for food. Our waitress, a girl fourteen or fifteen years old, repeatedly asked us, "*¿Tiene monedas de su país?*"— Do you have coins from your country? Then, after the drunk teenagers got up and staggered outside, she locked the door and braced it with two chairs. One of the drunks shouted at us from the other side of the barricaded door. The four of us gringos finished our meal, lingered in the restaurant, and left only when the shouting ceased. We walked back to our hotel. I felt relieved to disengage from the group.

I took a long time falling asleep that night despite severe fatigue. My throbbing knees disrupted me, though less so than my throbbing mind. I couldn't shake my bewilderment about the day's events. My recollections of walking through Chavín's dark passageways continued to disturb me. Encountering the ancient images had literally sickened me. To find bats, serpents, and a jaguar-faced god greeting me where the hallways met! The weak lantern light and the flashlight's jumpy beam made the stone faces shift as if alive. The *lanzón*: full of teeth, claws, and multitudinous eyes, this image alarmed me more than any ancient idol I'd ever seen. But why? Was my visceral response a result of the monolith's own properties? Could my physical state—fatigued, pained, agitated—explain my dizziness and revulsion? Could my dislike for my companions and my unease in their presence have heightened my already tense state of mind? Or was it possible that the *lanzón* itself, its origins and its nature, possessed some kind of inherent negativity? Ever since my teens, when I'd heard hippies refer to the "vibrations" and "auras" they ascribed to various objects, I had dismissed these notions as New Age hooey. Had I been too quick to brush off these notions? Perhaps an ancient stone could have a presence, an essence. If not exactly evil, then perhaps *chthonic*—earthy, earthly in the deepest sense of the word.

These thoughts plagued me for hours. At some point I fell asleep.

I AWOKE TO FIND THE MORNING dark and cloudy, rain falling, though the sky had been clear the night before. Somehow I had slept fairly well, which surprised me, especially since I had roused at one point on hearing someone pound on the hotel door—perhaps the same trouble-making teenager at the restaurant?—until the hotel's half-senile owner shouted at the tosspot in Quechua and convinced him to leave. My disquiet lingered, though I felt relieved to find my knees less swollen than the day before. I also felt my energy surge when I grasped that I would soon leave Chavín, return to Huaraz, and disengage from Peter and his friends.

On stepping out of the hotel and walking over to the Plaza de Armas, I learned that cargo trucks routinely drive west from Chavín and cross a pass into the Callejón de Huaylas. If I'd known about that route earlier, I could have spared myself three days of my companions' presence. The plus side: now I wouldn't have to walk the whole way back with them. I quickly managed to locate a Huaraz-bound truck. I arranged for the ride with the *chofer*, who told me to come back in an hour; then I joined the others for breakfast at a new restaurant they'd discovered. After eating, we returned to the Plaza de Armas, climbed up the truck's slatted wooden side into the cargo box, and nestled in among the gunny sacks of potatoes, onions, and apples heaped there. Five or six *campesinos* joined us on the pile of produce. The truck set off. We zigzagged up the mountain road; the *puna* opened up around us; and we proceeded to the pass, where a crude, unlighted tunnel crossed through the ridge into the Callejón de Huaylas. Then we worked our way down a sequence of alarmingly steep hairpin turns until we reached the valley floor. On the wider, less-steep main road we proceeded to the town of Catac. There Peter and I, leaving Dave and Jan on the truck, switched to a local bus. During our descent toward Huaraz, I felt alternating waves of impatience and serenity. The weather somehow reflected my mood: scudding clouds and tassels of rain suspended over the massive valley.

In this way the trek to Chavín concluded. I found Scott at our Huaraz hotel and discovered with relief that although he remained sick, he had coped adequately while alone and was starting to recover. I myself felt physically better, too—less exhausted, less achy. Returning to a larger town boosted my spirits. Although I felt crestfallen when Peter announced his plan to linger in Huaraz with Scott and me, I knew I would now have far more options for avoiding him. My mood lifted.

Scott and I left Huaraz later that week. We planned to spend a few days in Lima, then proceed south to Cuzco. Mercifully, Peter had preceded us after all—he planned to meet up with some *cocaineros* in the capital to close a drug deal—and his departure granted Scott and me an early release from his company.

THROUGH THE DECADES since my visit to Chavín, I have pondered my trip there and what I experienced in the ruins. Archaeological research since the late 1970's has revealed many aspects of the place and has clarified the nature of the ancient culture whose members built the religious site. Dr. John Rick's excavations, especially, have illuminated significant issues. Starting in the 1990's, Rick and his associates excavated not only burial platforms and ceremonial plazas; they also discovered a remarkable maze of underground galleries beneath the ceremonial complex. Their findings have helped to solidify understanding of Chavín's role as a cultural and religious center. Throughout the site they have found pottery, relics, ceremonial objects, so-called strombus (conch) trumpets, and idols. These and other artifacts have cast light on many features of the site, including the *lanzón*, the five-meter-tall monolith that depicts the Chavín culture's supreme god: the jaguar-headed, snake-haired, wildly fanged human that I had faced and had found so alarming at the intersection of underground passageways.

Based on these discoveries, John Rick's most radical notion is that the layout of Chavín, as well as the artifacts found there, strongly suggest an evangelical purpose: to convert the uninitiated. The labyrinth of tunnels and chambers appear to have been pathways to an inner sanctum. Also suggestive is the discovery of shiny coal "mirrors" that probably allowed the priestly elite to reflect sunlight into the tunnels. In addition, drainage canals hint at the possibility that priests and their acolytes ducted running water into the chambers to create loud, disorienting sound effects. How did these sensory barrages affect the people who experienced them? Dr. Rick speculates that initiation rites subjected pilgrims to sights and sounds that would overwhelm, confuse, and influence them. Using the maze of passageways as a disorienting venue, the priestly elite manipulated light and sound, immersing supplicants in a participatory *son et lumière* experience. The rituals would probably have started with novices ingesting a hallucinogenic substance derived from the San Pedro cactus. As the initiates worked their way through the dark, cramped hallways, the sound of conch trumpets echoed around them from unseen sources. Water roared through canals beneath their feet or even overhead, producing bizarre noises that the drugs would have intensified. Mirrors placed in ventilation ducts to reflect the sun would have poured brilliant shafts of light into the subterranean hallways, perhaps to be blocked abruptly at crucial moments, immersing the supplicants in total darkness. By the time the subjects emerged from the chambers, staggering and stunned, the experience would have changed their perspective forever. "The priest-elite of Chavín," Dr. Rick has written, "seem to have been creating a new sensory environment in which belief in the normal world is suspended, and assertions of otherworldliness [by] these religious authorities would have been made credible."

I've read about John Rick's discoveries in archaeological journals, and I find his theories plausible. The artifacts that he and his team have unearthed, as well as their further excavations of the galleries, make a strong case for Chavín having been a pilgrimage center. What, then, does this research mean about my own experience? Had I become an inadvertent pilgrim when I entered the dark hallways? Had I done obeisance to the ancient jaguar god? When I felt physically ill at the sight of this god's many-eyed, multi-fanged visage, had I grasped some kind of *mysterium tremendum*? Typical of my always-ambivalent, always-skeptical responses to such experiences—to almost all experiences—I don't know. Something happened. Something intense. Something complex, inchoate, bizarre. But I'm not sure what. I'm not sure why. Was it possible that my fatigue and physical discomfort, including the early symptoms of a rheumatoid condition, predisposed me toward agitation? Was it possible, too, that my worries about Peter's drug deals and the risk of guilt by association had left me feeling hyper-alert? Or that my unnerving encounter with the *campesino* on our trek's first night—the landowner who implied that I myself might be a henchman of the devil—might have fostered primordial anxieties? These and other concerns may have set the stage for my gut-wrenching, sweat-drenching response deep in Chavín's subterranean Holy of Holies. In any case, it seems that even absent the once-loud rushing water, the once-bright reflected light, the once-unnerving conch trumpets' blare, and the once-psychedelic effects of the San Pedro cactus: absent of all these factors, I had still suffered the effects, or perhaps benefited from the effects, of the long-dead priests' evangelical gambits. Or perhaps—to put the situation less charitably—I had simply ended up like Adela Quested, the young schoolmistress in E. M. Forster's *A Passage to India*, who enters an ancient cave, suffers disorientation and anxiety inside its void, and emerges shaken but unsure of what she had experienced.

There's a further aspect of the process I've undertaken toward understanding what happened to me early in July of 1977—a dose not of psychedelics but of ambiguity.

In the mid-1990's, while doing further research about Andean cultures, I stumbled on this passage in a recent guidebook: "Here [in the ruins of Chavín], at the intersection of crossing passageways, was discovered the large monolithic dagger stone, the *lanzón*. The original is now in Lima; however, a full-sized replica effectively occupies its place." I stopped reading. I paused. I went back to the start of the paragraph and reread it. " . . . *a full-sized replica* . . . " The realization hit me like a slap. *I had been spooked by a replica*. The effigy that had induced nausea, chills, and malaise inside the subterranean passage was a fake. A well-wrought fake—but a fake all the same.

What did this mean, to be spooked by a fake? Was my reaction pointless, ridiculous, silly? Had I become upset over something that wasn't "real"? If I had felt nausea, chills, and malaise on seeing the actual *lanzón* rather than a replica, would that have been a more legitimate experience? Maybe, but maybe not. An African American seeing a noose dangle from a tree, or even seeing a sketch or a photograph of a noose-dangling tree, would have every reason to feel sickened and appalled even though that specific tree might never have been the site of an actual lynching. A Jew would have every reason to feel appalled and sickened upon seeing a wrought iron gate bearing the slogan ARBEIT MACHT FREI—even if the gate were only a replica.

Indeed, any feeling person, whether African American, Jewish, or of any other background, would rightly feel revulsion and dread toward these icons of cruelty and hatred whether the objects were "real" or "fake." Why shouldn't I have felt unnerved and sickened on seeing chthonic imagery that felt threatening despite the bats, snakes, and jaguars being only a twentieth-century stonemason's mimicry of the ancient stela? The stone itself struck me as inherently, almost radiantly evil. Yet it wasn't. It was just a stone.

I had suffered the fearsome presence of a dead god, or of a dead god's image. But perhaps the fear I felt toward what seemed inchoate evil, as well as the struggle I fought in response, wasn't deep inside Chavín's ruins after all. In the words of Mahatma Gandhi, "The only devils in this world are those running around in our own hearts, and that is where all our battles should be fought."

ROTAS-SATOR? SATOR-ROTAS!

Words are the exoskeletons of thoughts. Words are the hammers we use for pounding thoughts into blades. Words are the torches we toss into the air like circus jugglers. Words are the swamps our thoughts wander into and then struggle to escape. The so-called SATOR Square is one such skeleton, one such hammer, one such torch, one such swamp—above all a swamp, five words able to pull us in, trap us, and sink us deep.

Painted ROTAS-SATOR Acrostic," the plaque stated. "Dura-Europos, block E7, Temple of Azzanathkona, ca. A.D. 165-256." What I saw before me on a wall in the Yale University Art Gallery was a crude terra cotta tile, nine inches tall and eight inches wide. Roughly rectangular, this tile suggested the work of an amateur artisan, not a skilled craftsman or -woman. The surface was uneven, the lettering irregular. The words present, however, caught my attention at once.

```
R  O  T  A  S
O  P  E  R  A
T  E  N  E  T
A  R  E  P  O
S  A  T  O  R
```

The gallery's explanatory plaque provided this overview:

This graffito has five lines of text: ROTAS, OPERA, TENET, AREPO, SATOR. The arrangement forms a complex word puzzle (like a palindrome) that reads the same from left to right, right to left, top to bottom, and bottom to top). Three more examples of this acrostic were discovered at Dura-Europos, with others found around the ancient world. The earliest comes from Pompeii, destroyed in A.D. 79. There have been many attempts to interpret this puzzle, often attributing a Christian meaning to it. Other scholars believe it has Mithraic or other magical significance."

My visit to the gallery took place several years ago, when my wife and I had visited New Haven on a business trip. First-century acrostics weren't my top priority at the time. I photographed the tile, however, as well as the explanatory plaque, then shelved the issue somewhere in a dusty corner of my mind. Years passed. Revisiting my photos at some point, I resumed pondering the ROTAS-SATOR square and started reading articles and blog posts that describe and explain it.

One blogger, Jenny Kile, offers this conjecture about the square's meaning:

> Different translations have been suggested for the twenty-five letters. Most of the variations, problems, or contradictions with translation seem to arise from the only word of the five which is not a known Latin word: AREPO. Assuming AREPO to be a possible proper name, though, the most common reading of the square is "the farmer/ gardener (SATOR) AREPO holds (TENET) and works (OPERA) wheels (ROTAS)." (The gardener Arepo holds and works the wheels/plough.) [1]

On another site, an anonymous blogger speculates along the same lines:

The SATOR Square also forms a sentence, though its meaning is obscure. Possible translations of the phrase are "The sower Arepo holds the wheels with effort" or "The sower Arepo leads with his hand (work) the plough (wheels)," and "The Great Sower holds in his hand all works; all works the Great Sower holds in his hand." The word *arepo* is enigmatic, appearing nowhere else in Latin literature. Most of those who have studied the SATOR Square agree that it is a proper name, either an adaptation of a non-Latin word or most likely a name invented specifically for this sentence." [2]

BEYOND THE SQUARE'S ORIGINS in first-century Mediterranean culture, it's clear that members of non-pagan communities imposed their own meanings onto the ROTAS-SATOR acrostic. Christians, among others, seem to have found the square compelling. Sandra Sweeny Silver, a writer and historian who maintains a blog called earlychurchhistory.org, notes that "nothing represented in Christian art means only what is represented," and she explains the square in light of that assumption: "The obvious meaning of the Sator Square to a Christian would have been Jesus' Parable of the Sower in Matthew 13:3-9, when He likened the spreading of the word of the kingdom of God to a farmer who sows seeds. Christians were spiritual farmers spreading the seeds of the Evangel, the Good News." Silver states that beyond the sower-of-seeds imagery reside further wordplay and further symbolism: "[H]idden in the Sator Square is an anagram when positioned in the form of a cross. By rearranging the 25 letters, a new phrase, extremely beloved by Christians down through the ages, is formed":

```
              P
              A
        A  T  O
              E
              R
P  A  T  E  R  N  O  S  T  E  R
              O
              S
        O  T  A
              E
              R
```

Silver's explanation:

> *Pater Noster* ("Our Father") is the beginning of The Lord's Prayer in Latin. The 25 letters arranged in this cross fashion say "Our Father" twice, vertically and horizontally, with two "A's" and two "O's" left over and placed as palindromes. "A" and "O" are the first and the last letters in the Greek alphabet and mean "Alpha, the Beginning" and "Omega, the End." Jesus called Himself the First and the Last in Revelation 1:8: "I am the Alpha and Omega . . . who is and who was and who is to come, the Almighty." [3]

In defense of this interpretation, Silver notes that what she calls "the Pater Noster square" appears in Roman ruins as early as the late 60's CE; at the Dura-Europos site in Syria; on the door of the Abbey of St. Peter ad Oratorium, built c. 752CE near Capestrano, Italy; in a c.-820-vintage Carolingian bible; on the masonry of the Church of St. Laurent, near Ardeche, France; in the castle keep of Loches, France; and on a second-century pottery shard unearthed in Manchester, England. "The very early appearance of the Sator Square," Silver writes, along with its geographical reach and the centuries of use, "attest to its popularity and to the power of its message, no matter how artfully encrypted it was."

Maybe so. But is "its message" truly the story that this word square relates? Do the five words tell an acrostic parable? Or does the alignment of ROTAS, OPERA, TENET, AREPO, SATOR add up to little more than a clever verbal sequence? Or, to ask the question by means of a comparison: if humans living 2,000 years in the future unearth a plaque bearing the words A MAN, A PLAN, A CANAL, PANAMA!, will these palindrome-speculators ascribe profound significance to the inscription? Will they speculate about a twentieth-century cult and the mysterious hero at its heart? Perhaps they will. The human quest for meaning drives members of our species to find hidden significance among words as eagerly as we perceive faces and animal shapes in the clouds. So, too, might people find occult meanings in other palindromes:

- DID I DO, O GOD—DID I AS I SAID I'D DO? GOOD! I DID.

- ARE WE NOT DRAWN ONWARD TO NEW ERA?

- REVERED NOW, I LIVE ON. O, DID I DO NO EVIL, I WONDER, EVER?

In short, the human appetite for meaning often prompts us to find more sustenance than is actually present. The ROTAS-SATOR square may have occult significance . . . but perhaps it doesn't. Perhaps it's just some words on a plaque. Perhaps it's little more than a first-century Roman's morsel of verbal cleverness. Who devised it? A linguist, a poet, a rhetorician? A thoughtful artisan braiding words in her mind while weaving cloth on her loom? Or perhaps two smart teenage boys taking a break from their tutor, Pedanticus, and his strict lessons:

> **Lucius:** *Non vis videre, quod vere mirabile?* ["Wanna see something really amazing?"]
>
> **Celsus:** *Noli mihi molestus esse! Lectio sum occupatus.* ["Don't bug me! I'm busy reading."]

Lucius: *Hic erit esto mansuetus, promitto.* ["This'll be quick, I promise."]

Celsus: *Bene . . .* ["Well . . ."]

Lucius: *Videre? Vos lego verba in omnem partem flecterentur.* ["See? You can read the words in any direction."]

Celsus: [now examining his pal's word square]: *O Iovi! Hic est valde infigo!* ["By Jupiter! This is way cool!"]

Then Pedanticus, ordering his students back to work, notices the wax tablet on which Lucius has inscribed some words with his stylus. *"Quid hoc est?"* he asks angrily, confiscating the tablet.

"Nihil!" protests the schoolboy.

Examining the inscription, Pedanticus finds his magisterial fury transmuting itself into curiosity. The boy has devised something clever. Beyond clever: strange. Strange enough that the tutor immediately grasps that his hands hold something remarkable, something resonant, something certain to impress everyone who sees it . . . everyone to whom Pedanticus himself will now show it.

The rest is verbal history. Our species finds significance everywhere. Even where it's absent.

Or, as another palindrome states:

IN WORD SALAD, ALAS, DROWN I.

The Snow Man

What does it mean to be lost? Does being lost presuppose not knowing where you are? What if you know exactly where you are, know exactly what you must do to go somewhere else, but are helpless to move forward? What if you have no agency? What if despite your best intentions you can't save yourself from stasis, helplessness, and—if worse comes to worst—doom?

Some years ago I traveled to my home state, Colorado, to visit friends and to participate in several literacy-promotion events at public schools in Denver. I also took advantage of this trip to go hiking in the Rockies. I had enjoyed this pastime since early boyhood, had become an avid camper and mountaineer during my teens, and had continued to hike and climb in many parts of North and South America during the decades since then. Moving to the Northeast in 1982, getting married in 1985, and then focusing on parenthood and career had limited my opportunities for the outdoor adventures I had pursued earlier. All the better, then, to return now and then to my old stomping grounds, as I did during this Colorado trip. That May, once I had finished my school visits, I headed up to the Breckenridge area for a solo climb.

My goal: Quandary Peak. This mountain is a Fourteener, one of the fifty-four in Colorado with an altitude of 14,000 feet or higher; and, like many in its class, Quandary is tall but not a technically difficult climb. It's essentially just a huge pile of granite boulders, slabs, and rubble. A successful ascent demands little more than good legs, good lungs, and some degree of patience. The weather is the only other significant variable. Winter in the Rocky Mountains is often harsh; spring and autumn are unpredictable; and summer is usually pleasant, even beautiful, but can present rapid temperature fluctuations and violent thunderstorms. I had climbed Quandary twice before, as well as dozens of other peaks in Colorado, in each of several seasons. The only challenge I expected this time around was the snowpack. May is still early spring in the Rockies, and much or most of the winter snowpack wouldn't have melted yet. It's not uncommon for ten, fifteen, or even twenty feet of snow to pile up at higher elevations in the Rockies between September and May, and the accumulation can linger well into the summer months. On approaching Quandary, I saw that the peak was still heavily cloaked in white. I assumed, however, that my early start would prevent any major problems during the climb.

This assumption proved to be accurate. I parked my rental car at the base of the mountain, slogged my way upward, and reached the summit without difficulty about two hours later. Except for three young men present—undergraduates from the Colorado School of Mines—I had the mountain to myself. The views were splendid from the top: a three-hundred-sixty-degree panorama of snow-capped peaks extending to a horizon at least a hundred miles away. The college guys asked if I would take a snapshot of them, which I did. They returned the favor with my own camera. I still have the photo of myself posing up there, clearly content and comfortable as I stood with the precipice a few feet behind me, the temperature so warm by ten a.m. that I had stripped down to jeans and turtleneck. After chatting with me for twenty or thirty minutes, the students then left the summit by plunging down the steep south face of the mountain, a technique called the standing *glissade*—essentially skiing without skis down the snowy slope. I had used this technique myself on many mountains. It's a quick way to descend from a peak under certain conditions; when used judiciously, it's often safer than descending more slowly. The main safety variable comes from having an ice axe in hand to use as an "arrest" device if the slide gets out of control. I had considered this exit strategy myself on Quandary. Unfortunately, I hadn't brought my own ice axe with me to Colorado, nor had I been able to obtain one in Denver before setting out on my little expedition, so I had assumed from the start that I couldn't risk a glissade off the mountain. I would need to retrace my steps instead.

The early phase of this retreat went well. I simply followed my own path along the dazzling white ridge of the mountain; I worked my way down Quandary's ramp-like slope; and, predictably, I made faster progress than during my ascent. Soon I was almost two-thirds of the way to the mountain's base. So far, so good. I was scarcely exerting myself, and the sixty-degree air temperature felt wonderful. Unfortunately, that warmth soon became a problem. During the hours of my ascent and my unexpected hangout time with the college students, the snowpack had softened. What had been as hard as concrete had now grown mushy. Worse than mushy: slushy. I soon found myself ankle-deep in snow as soft and wet as a Sno-Cone. Even so, I didn't feel concerned. My boots might get wet, I noted, but under the conditions present—warm weather and a short hike—I wouldn't suffer the risk of frostbite. I would surely reach the car in an hour or so.

I DIDN'T. The farther I descended, the more I floundered. Soon I was knee-deep in snow. Sometimes I sank even deeper—up to my hips, my waist, my chest. The situation grew alarming. I found that making any progress at all was awkward, laborious, and often counterproductive. Sometimes I would slog just a few steps, then bog down again. I started to wonder how deep I might go. In snowpack ten or fifteen feet deep, would I sink all the way to solid ground? Even if I sank only far enough that the surface was a foot or so over my head, what would happen to me? I had some snack items in my daypack—grain bars and chocolate—so I wouldn't have to cope with hunger

. . . at least for a while. I wouldn't die of thirst with all that snow around me. I would be able to breathe, given the open air overhead. Staying warm would be another matter: I would surely be subject to rapid chilling down there in my private icebox. Hypothermia might well become a serious threat. As I made repeated attempts to wallow my way out of the snowy morass, and as I floundered time after time, digging a series of inadvertent foxholes, I started to see what I was facing. To be alone on that huge expanse now seemed far less appealing than it had just a short while earlier.

At one point, standing there up to my armpits and gazing out across the brilliant, almost metallic glare of Quandary Peak, I realized that I was the only warm thing present. Everything around me consisted of tiny bits of ice. I felt as if I'd been cast overboard into a sea of snow. A twenty-minute drive north of where I stood at that moment, tourists were no doubt lingering over lunch in the chic restaurants down in Breckenridge. Neither that town nor anything else of human origin was visible to me now; and if it had been, its proximity would have made no difference. I couldn't see those people. I couldn't reach them. I may as well have been living in another country or even on another planet. What time was it, anyway? Late morning? Early afternoon? I glanced at my watch: eleven thirty.

It occurred to me that if nothing else, I could probably solve my problem—my Quandary, so to speak—simply by standing there for a long time. The sun would traverse the sky and would eventually set beyond the western expanse of peaks I had admired from the summit. Night would fall. The temperature would drop. The slushy snow all around me would cool, congeal, and harden once again. Patience would allow me to escape: I could eventually climb out of my pit onto a surface of the same tarmac-hard consistency present earlier that morning. But how many hours would these changes require? Eight, ten, twelve? And as the snowpack solidified again, how low would my body temperature drop during half a day of standing there while waiting for my exit ramp to solidify? Although I now grasped the likelihood of an eventual exit, I grew more and more concerned about the risk of hypothermia as I contemplated a long wait in the snow.

BASED ON MY DILEMMA, here are some issues that I recommend as objects of contemplation to anyone stuck up to his or her collarbone in a snowfield:

> **The abundance of snow.** There's a lot of snow in the world. And, as we all learned during childhood, *no two flakes are alike*. (Who, tell me, performed the comprehensive, flake-by-flake comparison of all snowfalls throughout the planet's entire history, thus determining the truth of this standard assumption? That has never been revealed. Neither has the methodology necessary to complete that process.) In terms of Quandary Peak, which has a surface area of approximately eighteen square kilometers, an average depth of four meters of snowpack would add up to about 72,000 cubic meters of white stuff. Small wonder that finding yourself embedded in the snowfield might leave you feeling stuck.

> **The ironies of modern telecommunications.** You have a cell phone in your daypack, but attempting to use it quickly presents you with the dead end you've feared: *No Signal*. The skiers and tourists in Breckenridge will be yakking away on their phones and texting photos of their restaurant meals, but your chances of connecting with the Summit County 911 service and thus reaching the local backcountry rescue team are basically zip.

> **Various psychosocial aspects of getting lost in the wilderness.** The only option that might suddenly

change your situation would be the arrival of one or more off-season hikers as they trek up the mountainside. That possibility isn't out of the question, but it doesn't seem likely at this time of day. It's the middle of the week during the off season, and most climbers start out in the morning anyway. You feel surprisingly ambivalent about the possibility of being "rescued." If you were actually *in extremis*—sinking deeper and deeper into the snow, perhaps, or suffering from early-stage hypothermia—your thoughts would be more straightforward. But to have a party of hikers come snowshoeing up the slope and finding you stuck but not yet in dire distress: all in all, you prefer to bide your time a while longer.

The inevitability of retrospective self-retribution. Nevertheless, you soon start kicking yourself for the miscalculations that have landed you here. You're an experienced hiker and mountaineer, but you've violated the first rule of back-country travel: never travel alone. That you have hiked in this area for almost five decades and have climbed Quandary Peak twice before provides no excuse. You're aware that all hikers should assess the specific conditions for each hike. Having set aside years of experience and having forgotten how dramatically snowpack can change, you are now taking the consequences.

The likelihood of marital freakout. If this dilemma continues much longer, your wife will be worried sick. *Where are you, anyway? Why haven't you called yet?* Since she knows you're on a backcountry hike, she'll be wondering if you've suffered an accident on the mountain. Maybe a car wreck on the drive back to Denver? A heart attack? You've put her in a terrible position. Your inability to resolve this dilemma leads to genuine anxiety on her behalf . . . not to mention some degree of concern that once you make it back to civilization and phone home—assuming, of course, that you succeed in getting out—she will be not just relieved but also (appropriately) angry.

The big picture. You're still up to your sternocleidomastoids in snow. As far as you can tell, you're the only human being on the entire mountain. Nothing anywhere around you has any awareness of your presence, much less any interest in whether you live or die. Not since your foolish but non-calamitous solo trek in the north-central Peruvian Andes back in 1971—an experience now more than thirty years behind you, thus handily written off as youthful bravura—have you found yourself in such unforgiving isolation. To complicate matters, you are under-equipped and less than adequately attired for the conditions; you have very little subcutaneous fat on your body, ergo no insulation at all; and you're chilling rapidly. This is Not a Good Situation.

THESE AND OTHER THOUGHTS, analyses, conjectures, worries, ruminations, fantasies, and speculative decision trees sprouted, grew, and branched throughout my mind for a long time. If the circumstances had deteriorated—if clouds had moved in, for instance, and rain had started falling—I would have shifted into yet more alarmist, even paranoid modes of thinking. Was the situation stable, thus justifying a measured response? Maybe so. I certainly wasn't facing a crisis on the level of what Aron Ralston had faced recently, when, during his solo trek in Canyonlands National Park, a loose boulder pinned his right arm to the canyon wall he was climbing, a dilemma that prompted him to conclude after several days of isolation that he could survive only by amputating his own arm as a first step in making his escape. Nothing in my situation bore any resemblance to that level of emergency.

All the same, I felt as fully and perhaps eternally stuck in this snowy hole as Farinata in his infernal sarcophagus: no way out. (Even Farinata benefited from visitors now and then, as when Dante and Virgil stopped by for a friendly chat.)

AT SOME POINT during the tedious minutes of standing in my chilly foxhole, I examined my surroundings more closely. I confirmed that I was completely surrounded by snowpack. No outcroppings of granite had been exposed yet as the winter's accumulations receded, which left me without any alternate surface to use as an exit ramp. I noticed patches of scrub oak, however, only a few dozen yards downhill from where I stood. These thickets are typical of Colorado's alpine ecosystems: a species of shrub that can survive at higher altitudes than trees. The scrub oak wouldn't offer any assistance to me as such, but the bushes suggested that the snow might be shallower down there than I'd expected: branches of this species generally grow about five or six feet tall. Spotting them gave me hope. If I could just work my way down there, perhaps I could wallow further with less difficulty. I also noticed that the scrub oak bushes cast shadows onto the snow massed between them, which might create a cooler, less-soft surface for me to walk on.

One other insight: my pack, which I had taken off and placed at the rim of my foxhole, rested there without sinking. It weighed just fifteen pounds or so—about a seventh of my body weight—so its remaining on the surface didn't surprise me. Seeing it there prompted me to ponder another aspect of the situation. Bantamweight though I may be, my one hundred eighteen pounds all bear down on the soles of my hiking boots. What if I could distribute my bulk more evenly? Would the snow support me? If I could lie on the surface and somehow move downhill while stretched out, could I work my way over to the alpine shrubbery? This gambit would be the equivalent of what I've heard that people should do when caught in quicksand: ease onto your back, float, and slowly "swim" to safety. It seemed worth a try.

What followed was a laborious, strenuous, ungainly, and often ridiculous effort to work my way downhill. Just climbing out of the foxhole took four or five minutes. My next steps after that weren't auspicious: all I did was sink in again and climb out, sink in and climb out, over and over. I considered scrapping the whole effort and reverting to Plan A: waiting. Eventually, however, I managed to make the method work. I didn't swim, exactly, so much as purposefully flounder. Motions appropriate to water or even quicksand, such as kicking and stroking, weren't effective. Slithering only dug me in again. Anything that disturbed the surface of the snow tended to be counterproductive. Rolling, however: *rolling* had possibilities.

My backpack proved to be a problem until I discovered that holding it over my head shifted its weight away from me and avoided impeding my motion. Progress was unpredictable and awkward. Sometimes I gained only a foot or two before sinking. Sometimes I gained a few yards. Soon my jeans and jacket were soaked—not a good development. Yet a sustained effort showed that I would succeed in reaching the stand of scrub oak. Then surely my struggle would ease. That wasn't entirely true, as the snow between the shrubs proved no more solid than all the rest. I could pull myself forward by grasping the branches, however, and doing so helped me progress from one patch to another.

A long time later—what seemed at least three or four hours—I succeeded in working my way down to timberline. There, among the pines and spruces, I reached an expanse of snow that had been covered by trees' shadows throughout the morning and afternoon hours. The surface underfoot was soft but able to sustain my weight. What a luxury: to walk upright! To take steps without plunging into the snow! Soon I could proceed at a normal place. I descended through the forest. Moving fast now—both to keep warm and to make up for lost time—I strode off the mountain and, feeling a huge sense of relief, succeeded in reaching my car.

I STOWED MY SOAKING-WET PACK in the trunk, changed into dry clothes, and prepared to leave the base of Quandary Peak. At some point I checked the time: not quite 1 p.m. Despite my perception of having floundered for many hours on the mountain, only about ninety minutes had passed since I first bogged down in the snow.

I returned to Breckenridge. I phoned Edith to tell her that I was fine despite the delay in calling. Since I had now completed everything scheduled for my week in Colorado, I drove back to Denver for my return flight to the New York metro area.

Later, on the plane, I considered my quandary on Quandary. Getting mired on the slope hadn't come close to becoming a near-death experience; all the same, it was a disturbing crisis that could have gotten much worse before it got any better. I love snow, but finding myself stuck in it up to my armpits gave me too much of a good thing. And the strangeness of looking out at the world—at the vast curve of the mountainside, at the entire upper reaches of Breckenridge Valley, at the mountain range beyond, and at the perfect, empty dome of the sky above—had felt almost overwhelming. It's inevitable in such a place and at such a time to feel insignificant, almost non-existent. The inevitability of that sensation doesn't make it any easier. What, then, could I make of the jolt this experience had given me? Where should I "file" it?

I found myself turning back almost against my will to one of the greatest American poems, "The Snow Man," by Wallace Stevens, a poem that has long prompted me to regard Stevens as a closet Buddhist, or perhaps as someone who, despite his decades of living and working in the urban Northeast, at some point spent several hours contemplating the blankness of the universe while mired in crystalized water at timberline.

The Snow Man[1]

One must have a mind of winter
To regard the frost and the boughs
Of the pine-trees crusted with snow;

And have been cold a long time
To behold the junipers shagged with ice,
The spruces rough in the distant glitter

Of the January sun; and not to think
Of any misery in the sound of the wind,
In the sound of a few leaves,

Which is the sound of the land
Full of the same wind
That is blowing in the same bare place

For the listener, who listens in the snow,
And, nothing himself, beholds
Nothing that is not there and the nothing that is.

Mi Gringo

The incident of the little girl's head wound started without warning or drama. One of the teenage members of the Espinosa family, who lived next door to my hosts, Jesús and Alejandra Rivera, entered the Riveras' compound and descended the concrete steps to the patio. I happened to be sitting there after the midday meal. The teenager was Guadalupe, nicknamed La Coica, age thirteen. Jesús and Alejandra must have been somewhere else, and their twenty-year-old son, Pepe, was off at the teachers' academy, so I interacted with La Coica before anyone else. *"¿Tienes una curita?"* she asked me. Do you have a band-aid?

"Sí, claro," I answered—yes, of course. I went to the bedroom I shared with Pepe, found my first aid kit, removed a couple of band-aids, and returned to the courtyard.

La Coica took them shyly. "Do you have anything bigger?"

"How much bigger?"

She held her index fingers five inches apart.

At this point I grew concerned. "What's it for?" I asked, wondering why she needed such a large dressing.

La Coica now described her youngest sister's accident. Remedios, age four, had fallen off a crude wooden ladder that the Espinosa family used instead of a staircase at the back of their house. On striking the ground, Remedios had gashed open her forehead. I knew even without any paramedical training that this accident would require more than just a band-aid. I went upstairs, found Jesús where he was arranging materials for our masonry project, and explained the situation. He and I then followed La Coica to the Espinosa's house next door.

When we entered the family's cramped, dimly lit front room, we found Remedios sitting on her sister Margarita's lap, the little girl dazed and weepy, a nearly two-inch-long cut across the center of her forehead. The wound resembled a mouth, the lips puffy and drooling blood. Partly visible beyond the lips was a slick white surface that I realized with a jolt of alarm might be the surface of Remedios's skull. Watching me as I examined the girl were Macaria, age eight; Rogelio, the sisters' oldest brother, age twenty; and Ángela, their always-exhausted mother, age fifty but appearing fifteen or twenty years older. Everyone in the room was silent, uneasy, uncertain. I, too, felt unsure what to do. Twenty-one years old, I was merely a friend of the Espinosas' next-door in-laws—a foreigner visiting their Mexican *barrio*, a *gringo* with no medical knowledge. A year later, when I started working in hospitals, I acquired extensive first-aid skills, but during my stay with the Rivera family in 1971, I knew very little. I knew enough, however, to realize that Rogelio was now preparing to take a step that would make a bad situation much worse.

This handsome, muscular young man, whose curly black hair provided the only resemblance to his frail father, held a rag in one hand. The cloth looked wet and smelled oily. I could tell right off that he intended to wipe his little sister's wound with some kind of petrochemical.

"What are you doing?" I asked, surprising myself with my own bluntness.

"Cleaning the cut." His expression showed annoyance. Although I had often interacted pleasantly with his sisters during the two months of my stay so far, Rogelio had always seemed resentful of my presence in the neighborhood.

"What's the liquid?"

"Gasoline."

His words jolted me. "That won't help," I told him. "It's not a good antiseptic, and it'll prevent the wound from healing." I wasn't confident of these assertions, but I stated them anyway.

"So what should I do?" he asked, his words exclaiming more than asking.

I couldn't imagine Remedios's fate if she didn't get medical attention. "She needs a doctor."

Rogelio's expression now showed something like contempt. "A doctor. We can't afford a doctor."

I looked at each person in the room. Antonia's face was blank, as always—passive, weary, empty of expectations. Remedios looked blank in a different way: from shock, perhaps? Her sisters all looked anxious but unable to take action. Rogelio's features showed disgust and anger, as if he felt outraged that the little girl would cause everyone so much trouble. Jesús— small and fit at age forty-five, with brown skin and alert black eyes—watched me without judgment but with some kind of expectancy.

"I'll pay for it," I said impulsively.

I stepped away from everyone else to confer with Jesús. "This girl really needs help," I told him, "but it might cost quite a bit." He nodded grimly. We discussed the situation. His half-brother, Juan—Ángela's husband and the father of these children—was somewhere in town, probably at one of the local cantinas. Rogelio almost certainly had no money. His more responsible brothers, Antonio and Martín, were up north in Texas working as farm laborers to support the family. I told Jesús that I would help the Espinosas, given their tough circumstances. Once again he nodded.

In this way my involvement in the Espinosa family's crisis began. After I'd taped some gauze onto the little girl's forehead, five of us headed off to find the clinic—La Coica carrying Remedios, Jesús and Rogelio and I walking together ahead of them.

REMEDIOS'S ACCIDENT and the resulting scalp wound presented a bizarre twist in a sequence of events that had unfolded smoothly until that afternoon. I had been living congenially with the Riveras for almost two months. This arrangement and the project at its center were part of a plan that my parents and I had devised with Jesús and Alejandra, a couple we had met during a visit to Mexico fourteen years earlier and with whom we had remained close ever since. The plan: I would spend three months with the Riveras. They would provide lodging and meals, introduce me to their way of life, show me their town and the surrounding area, and help me improve my Spanish. In exchange, I would take part in *la obra*, a construction project intended to expand the Riveras' three little rooms into a much larger, more comfortable six-room house. Our families had discussed the possibility of this arrangement for years, but only in recent months had it become a real option. Having decided to take a gap year following my first two years of college, and having grown strong enough to handle the rigors of construction work, I was now both available and ready to do strenuous manual labor. *La obra* would entail building a brick and concrete house using only hand tools.

Up to that point, the Riveras had lived in their few small rooms. Jesús and Alejandra slept in the bedroom. Pepe slept on a sofa in the living room. The other room was a simple kitchen with two tables, a pair of tabletop gas burners, some shelves, an old refrigerator, and a water tank. The rooms stood apart from one another, each set in a corner of the property facing the irregularly shaped courtyard and surrounded by a brick wall. All three rooms were damp, dark, and drafty. The living room had a concrete lid; the bedroom and kitchen were roofed with reddish clay tiles. According to Julio, the kitchen leaked during rainstorms. Alejandra's health suffered as a result of these conditions, and all three family members felt frustrated by the lack of space. The Riveras had dreamed for years of building a larger house on their property. Know-how wasn't the problem. Jesús, extensively trained as a brick mason, could do the most technical work himself. The problem was paying for materials. Given Mexico's stagnant economy at that time, the Riveras were so under-employed that saving money for the bricks and mortar had proved impossible. My parents had discussed the situation with them through correspondence over several years; my mother, a Mexican immigrant to the U.S. who had become fast friends with Alejandra when they first met in 1957, had offered to fund the project; and now, after arranging for my extended visit to the Riveras' household, Jesús and Alejandra had access to sufficient funds that they could undertake the project. I had arrived in early April to participate in the work. (Pepe, enrolled in a rigorous teacher-training program, was essentially sidelined.) The project had gone well. Building brick walls and concrete pillars had been an exhausting but compelling experience for me. Each day brought new skills and a tangible sense of accomplishment as the new house took shape. Nothing had gone wrong.

In addition to the construction work, I had enjoyed getting to know the Riveras, their relatives, and their neighbors. I had also become fascinated by the surrounding community. Their town, one of twenty-seven UNESCO World Heritage Sites in Mexico, is picturesque, popular with tourists, and, given its popularity, more affluent than most in the region. As I discovered in 1971, however, impoverished barrios surrounded the well-preserved colonial-era *centro histórico*. Jesus, Alejandra, and Pepe lived in one of these poor neighborhoods; and, right next door, the Espinosa family eked out their even more marginal existence.

Several of the Riveras' other relatives lived in the area, and I met most of them during my stay that spring. Alejandra's sister and her husband owned a small farm at the far edge of town. One of Jesús's brothers, Aniseto, and two sisters, Carmen and Pancha, shared a house down the street. A half-brother, Juan Espinosa, lived with his family next door. This last household was the cluster of relatives that the Riveras interacted with most frequently.

I soon realized that my hosts felt deeply ambivalent about the Espinosas. When Alejandra first mentioned her brother-in-law, she made an unfamiliar but self-explanatory gesture: the thumb and little finger of her right hand extended, the three middle fingers curled toward the palm, the entire hand tipped toward her mouth like a bottle. *"A Juan le gusta mucho el tequila,"* she told me later. Juan really likes tequila. Beyond that, she and Jesús both held Juan in contempt for neglecting his family. Juan's wife, Ángela, had given birth to twelve children, of whom five had died, so that, as Ángela herself described the outcome to me at one point, "Now I have only seven." Given Juan's alcoholism and neglect as a father and husband, Angela was effectively the sole parent for this brood. The three oldest among her offspring were teenage sons. One of the boys, Rogelio, clearly took after his dad. During my three-month visit, I never once saw him doing work of any kind, though he often sat on a wall overlooking the *callejón*, where he played his guitar and serenaded the neighborhood. His brothers, Antonio and Martín, were much more industrious and were, in fact, the family's chief breadwinners. Jesús and Alejandra told me that these boys often traveled north to the U.S. border, crossed into Texas, worked as undocumented field hands, and earned money to send their mother. The other Espinosa kids were all girls. Among these were two teenagers, Guadalupe and Margarita; Macaria, age seven or eight; and Remedios, age four. I interacted just occasionally with most of these daughters. The exception was Macaria. Skinny and stick-legged, with a head of curly black hair and deep brown eyes, she visited the Rivera household frequently to serve as Alejandra's helper, for which the girl earned some pocket money and, more importantly, received more attention and affection from her aunt than she gained from her own mother.

In short, the family situation was complex. The whole neighborhood, I soon realized, was complex. When I first arrived, I had somehow imagined that the *barrio* would be a neighborly place. Poverty would unite the people here; they would look after one another. This expectation didn't hold true. People lived in close quarters—small homes wedged together all over the hillside—but they didn't interact much. Neighbors greeted one another in passing; they sometimes hung out and talked in the street (usually men with men, women with women); but otherwise they spent most of their time with their own families. Far from uniting people, poverty kept them apart. Each family's troubles were sufficient to demand its members' time and energy. Both Jesús and Alejandra described conflicts, rivalries, and resentments among the neighbors. Among the resentments were what they themselves felt toward Juan Espinosa.

ALTHOUGH I CHATTED SEVERAL TIMES each week with Macaria, I didn't speak often with her sisters. La Coica stopped by now and then to confer with Alejandra, but she and I said little to each other beyond *hola* and *hasta luego*. Small-town Mexican culture was still so traditional at the time that unrelated men and women often didn't interact much with one another. There was little or no reason for a twenty-one-year-old male to converse with a pre-teen girl, much less with a girl of preschool age who wasn't a relative. For this reason, I rarely talked to Remedios.

I recall one exception. During my several months with the Riveras, I sometimes watched the local kids play in the *callejón*. This narrow, unpaved alleyway was the closest thing they had to a playground. They also roamed about on the dusty, filthy, cluttered hillside that rose above the *barrio*. When running errands on foot, I either walked through the *callejón* before heading downhill or else skirted the hillside to take a different route into town. On those walks I sometimes crossed paths with the local kids at play. I saw quickly that they owned only a few store-bought toys. Some of the boys kicked a soccer ball back and forth, and once or twice I saw girls playing with cheap plastic dolls. Otherwise the kids improvised their playthings: little paper boats to float in puddles, swords made of sticks, slingshots whittled from forked tree branches, dolls assembled out of rags and string.

One afternoon, however, I found Macaria, Remedios, and a few other children flying tiny model airplanes. I did a double-take. How was this possible? How had they acquired such high-tech miniature devices? Each airplane, just an inch long, buzzed this way and that on a delicate tether.

"*¿Qué hacen, chiquitos?*" I asked, feeling baffled. What are you doing, kids?

"*Volando mayates,*" Macaria explained. Flying *mayates.*

Remedios too was flying her own little aircraft. The little girl held her arm out, allowing the plane to approach me on its tether.

"What are *mayates?*" I asked.

Now Remedios stared at me in disbelief, astonished that anyone could be so ignorant. "*Mayates* are—*mayates,*" she said.

Her plane veered toward me now, flying close enough for me to see it clearly. When I understood what I was seeing, I was amazed. This wasn't an airplane at all, but a beetle: metal-lic green, iridescent, roughly the size of an American quarter. Somehow each kid had caught one of these insects, looped a thread about its thorax, and coaxed it back into the air. A beau-tiful sight: Remedios smiling in delight as a *mayate* now buzzed around her, a live beetle orbiting its child-planet.

THE FIRST TRIP TO THE CLINIC resulted in a long walk, a protract-ed wait, and no medical care. La Coica glumly carried Reme-dios; Rogelio and Jesús and I preceded them. When the older sister encountered friends in the streets, they asked what had happened, and La Coica stopped to explain. Remedios looked about—stunned, speechless. If I'd known then what I learned during my hospital jobs starting just a few years later, I would have urged everyone to hurry up. Remedios might well have suffered a concussion. She might already be in shock. Why weren't we getting her down to the clinic faster? Instead, we tarried. Only after La Coica finished chatting did we proceed. Reaching the clinic at last, the staff members present listened to our explanation but wouldn't take action. No doctor was on duty, the receptionist told us, and the nurses present had no authority to do more than wash the wound. We waited a long time and received only brief attention. "Come back at four," the receptionist said. Discouraged, we left.

YEARS LATER, when I described my stay with the Riveras to various American friends, and especially when I explained how my family had funded the Riveras' construction project, a few of these friends criticized the whole venture. The notion that an affluent foreigner would arrive, bankroll the project, participate for a few months, and leave: this struck them as intrusive, even condescending. One left-leaning writer-friend, herself knowledgeable of Latin American history and of U.S. malfeasance in the region, expressed especially negative views: "It's like you were this mini-Peace Corps parachuting in to rescue the Third World from its backwardness."

"I wasn't rescuing the Third World," I protested. "My parents and I were helping some friends we had known for almost fourteen years."

"It still seems rather—*colonial.*"

"Would it have been better if I let them just live in their dark, cramped, leaky old house?"

"Of course not. But what you describe still sounds kind of offensive. You're the rich white guy who shows up to help the poor brown people."

I found her comments at best short-sighted. "I don't think the Riveras saw it that way."

"Maybe not."

"Besides, I'm Mexican-American."

"So what? In their eyes you're still a rich gringo."

After we sparred for a while on this topic, she backed off.

I realized later, however, that her objections had some validity, especially regarding the incident of Remedios and her accident.

≈ ≈ ≈

AFTER WORKING OUR WAY up the hillside to the Riveras's *barrio*, several of us rested together in the house belonging to Pancha, one of Jesús's sisters. Among us were La Coica, Remedios, and Jesús. Rogelio, having lost interest, had left. Remedios remained calm to a worrisome degree: surely no four-year-old would stay so quiet for so long unless suffering side effects from her fall. Or perhaps she was simply tired and scared, thus most at ease in her sister's arms. In any case, we lingered in Pancha's house. Then, unexpectedly, Juan arrived. His appearance startled me in the same way it had in the past: he seemed smaller up close than at a distance, much older than his fifty years, dressed in too-big jeans and a too-big western-style shirt, his hair disheveled, his teeth rotted or missing. Even before he spoke I could smell the odor of alcohol. He greeted Jesús and me but not the women present. He showed no concern about his young daughter. He had at least deigned to show up, however, which seemed a positive development.

We waited another hour in Pancha's little cottage, its walls cluttered with images of Christ and various saints. We spoke little. I was struck once again by the differences I had always sensed between Jesús's alertness and intelligence compared to Juan's dull, vague responses to everything. Then, around three-thirty, all of us except Pancha set off for the clinic: Remedios once again carrying Remedios while Jesús, Juan, and I led the way.

This time the hospital personnel accepted the little girl as a patient. La Coica accompanied her sister down the hallway. The girls' father showed no interest in being present for his youngest daughter's examination and treatment. Juan, Jesús, and I sat in the waiting area among other Mexicans. None of us spoke much. At some point we heard a sudden, brief scream—probably from Remedios when the doctor injected anesthetic into her forehead. Ten or fifteen minutes passed before La Coica emerged with her sister. Remedios looked teary but otherwise fine. A large gauze pad and white tape spanned her forehead. Then a nurse came out to explain that the doctor had found no signs of a skull fracture or any other head injury; he had simply cleaned, stitched, and bandaged the scalp wound. The nurse provided a prescription for an antibiotic that Remedios needed to take as a hedge against infection. She assured us that everything would be fine.

Next came the issue of payment. The charges added up to three hundred sixty pesos—approximately thirty dollars. In 1971, that amount was the equivalent of about $190 in 2019. Even without calculating the exchange rate, I knew that Juan, being both unemployed and inclined to spend his family's scant income on booze, couldn't afford the charges. Jesús and I glanced back and forth at each other and at Juan. I realized that I had to follow through—that I wanted to follow through—on my offer to cover the tab. I walked over to the clinic's *caja* and paid the bill. We left.

On the walk back to the *barrio*, we took a side trip to fill the prescription at a pharmacy near the *centro*. I paid for the antibiotics, which Juan then took and stuck in his jeans pocket. He thanked me for helping his family. He also asked suddenly, *¿Quieres un cono de fruta?"*—Would you like a fruit cone?—a tasty local snack.

"No thanks," I told him. "Jesús and I will be carrying loads of sand once we get back, and I'd better do the work on an empty stomach."

"How about a *refresco?"*

"No, but thank you anyway." Then, noticing how earnestly Jesús was staring at me, I realized that I'd missed the point I should have caught right off. Juan was offering his gratitude for my help. "Sure," I said, "that would be nice." The four of us detoured to a nearby snack shop, ordered sodas, and lingered in the shade. Remedios sat on La Coica's lap; the two girls shared a Fanta. The two other men and I each drank Coca-Cola. This denouement to the day's crisis seemed a far better outcome than I'd expected. Somehow I started feeling more and more uneasy, however, gradually realizing how oblivious I'd been, how much I'd focused on being the Espinosa family's benefactor. Maybe this brief stop for refreshments would satisfy Juan's desire to do something in return.

Then, while we sat near the café, he started pressing the point further. "*¿Quieres ver una verdadera cantina mexicana? ¿Conmigo?*" Would you like to see a real Mexican cantina? With me?

Given the Riveras' many comments about Juan's alcoholism—not to mention the stories Jesús had told me over the past months about the unpredictable, even dangerous nature of cantinas—I didn't feel eager. "Sorry," I told him, "but I don't drink."

"*¿No te gusta la cerveza?*" He sounded astonished: You don't like beer?

I looked to Jesús for guidance—some kind of nod, either yes or no, some kind of hint. He looked attentive but didn't nudge me one way or the other.

"Thanks," I told Juan, "maybe some other time. Jesús and I have to get back to work—all that sand to carry."

The conversation sputtered out. Juan looked more than a little disappointed. I felt uneasy but relieved when we set off again, climbed the hillside back to the *barrio,* and parted company when Juan and his daughters returned to their house, Jesús and I to the Riveras' compound.

IN THIS WAY THE EMERGENCY ENDED. Remedios suffered no infection or any other side effect from her head wound. Typical of a three-year-old child's robust immune system and powers of recovery, she healed quickly. Two days after the accident, I saw her playing energetically in the *callejón.* She remained shy in my presence but sometimes smiled when our eyes met. I learned some days later from Alejandra that Macaria had told her aunt something I found surprising: Remedios now referred to me as *mi gringo*—"my American."

More than surprising: amusing and touching. A lovely honor. But not just that, as I discovered over the next few days.

Interactions with Rogelio soon grew even more tense than before. When I encountered him, he either ignored me, behaved with exaggerated deference, or muttered at me as I passed. I rarely saw Juan, but on the rare occasions when we crossed paths, he acted uneasy or remote.

It didn't take me long to grasp that even though I'd helped the Espinosas—had saved one of their family members from a potentially severe medical problem, perhaps even from death by infection—appreciation wasn't the sum total of their response. I had taken actions far beyond their means. I had intruded upon, even usurped, Juan's and Rogelio's roles as their family's protectors. This would have caused resentment among most men in most cultures. In macho Mexico, I had committed a major sin. Precisely by helping Remedios, I had emasculated the little girl's father and brother.

When I hinted to Jesús and Alejandra that both Rogelio and Juan now acted rather distant, both of them offered reassurance.

"You did the right thing," Jesús said.

"Rogelio and Juan are both very proud," Alejandra added, "even though they don't have much to be proud about."

"You did the right thing," Jesús repeated.

TO CLARIFY ASPECTS of Remedios's medical condition back in 1971, I recently asked a friend of mine, Marcus Coxon, M.D., for his insights. Marcus is currently a family-medicine doctor, but an earlier phase of his career involved sixteen years of work as an emergency-room physician. What could he tell me about the injury that Remedios had suffered? Specifically, what would have happened if the girl's wound hadn't received treatment?

The biggest concern following blunt trauma to the head, he explained, wouldn't be the scalp laceration itself but, rather, the possibility of a skull fracture and a brain injury. He asked how far the girl had fallen, whether she had lost consciousness following the impact to her head, and whether she had manifested certain symptoms (dizziness, nausea, vomiting, and disorientation) afterwards. When I assured him that the clinic's doctor had examined Remedios, had asked her sister the relevant questions, and had determined that Remedios hadn't suffered a more serious head injury, Marcus and I moved on to discuss the wound itself. Given what I'd described, Marcus said, "Cleaning the wound with gasoline would have been a major problem." A petrochemical fluid would have prevented proper healing and, to make matters worse, would have been toxic to the body overall. What if the wound hadn't been cleaned with gasoline but had gone untreated? "It probably wouldn't have been fatal," Marcus told me, "but the wound would have healed poorly and would have resulted in an ugly scar." For proper healing, it would have needed to be stitched no later than twenty-four hours after the accident. Stitched or not stitched, was there a significant risk of infection? His response: "The scalp is so vascular that [wounds there] rarely lead to infection. But if it wasn't kept clean and cared for, and if there was a skull fracture, the girl could have suffered an infection or meningitis, perhaps leading to serious illness and maybe death." Absent underlying damage to the skull, however, Remedios probably would have survived. Overall, he concluded, "the greatest risk would have been disfigurement." Remedios's wound could have produced a large, conspicuous, mouth-shaped scar.

MY STAY WITH THE RIVERA FAMILY continued through the spring. Jesús and I persisted in our daily tasks of constructing the new rooms. We laid bricks to build the walls; we wired lengths of rebar into "spines" that would undergird the corner pillars; we encased these metal skeletons with scrap lumber; and, with assistance from two or three male teenage neighbors, we mixed and poured concrete to create the pillars themselves. Next steps involved setting up a complex wooden framework that would support concrete to create the roof for these new rooms. Later, in the Mexican equivalent of a barn raising, we mobilized a team of local guys to mix and pour several tons of cement, all of which we mixed by hand using only shovels, then carried to the upper level one bucketful at a time. I found these tasks more difficult, more exhausting, and somehow more satisfying than any other manual labor I had ever done before. By the time I left Mexico late that spring, the Riveras and I had succeeded in creating the house they had always wanted but had never fully believed they would ever own.

The months I spent with them were successful in this and other ways. Among other things, my stay with Jesús, Alejandra, and Pepe strengthened my friendship with them, as well as the bond between our two families. They expressed deep appreciation for my parents' financial assistance and for my contribution to the construction project; in turn, I felt deep gratitude for their generosity in hosting me, in explaining their life stories, and in teaching me so much about Mexican culture. I left feeling physically exhausted and emotionally elated.

Yet something gnawed at me. I knew that I hadn't handled some events during my stay with the greatest possible sensitivity. Despite being Mexican-American, I had often misunderstood aspects of my hosts' culture—their values, their modes of communication, their expectations and preferences. At age twenty-one, I hadn't experienced enough of the world to read their signals accurately. I had sometimes spoken bluntly in ways that rubbed against the formality and politeness inherent in Mexican culture. Jesús and Alejandra, always generous and gracious, had responded patiently to my missteps. In addition, they always appreciated what my parents and I were making possible for them. Was this two-family project "colonial"? Maybe so; maybe not. In any case, I believe that the risks we took together were sufficiently worthwhile as we collaborated to help their family attain a greater degree of safety and comfort.

What of the incident of Remedios—her accident, her scalp laceration, her need for medical treatment? Here again I probably didn't act with adequate grace when I intervened. At a minimum, I stepped on, perhaps trampled, Juan's and Rogelio's pride. Should I have backed off, then, even if doing so risked the little girl's wellbeing? Probably not. I had little choice but to take the steps I took. Years later, after working for a decade on hospital wards, and later still, while serving as a volunteer EMT, I realized that medical crises often require interventions that can seem abrasive, intrusive, even aggressive. I participated in emergency medical responses that involved arguing with patients or their family members and taking steps that may have seemed overbearing. At times people's sensitive feelings must be secondary to the tasks of diagnosis and treatment. Sometimes feelings must be ignored. As a result, the overall outcome of medical intervention may be positive but may leave a trail of resentments in its path. Sometimes intervention ends up messy. Under the circumstances I faced during Remedios's emergency, I probably misjudged, or under-thought, at least the aftermath. I didn't handle the situation right.

I RETURNED TO THE RIVERAS' TOWN for a brief reunion in 1983, exactly twelve years after my long stay with them. For several days during *Semana Santa*—Holy Week—I visited with Jesús, Alejandra, and Pepe to catch up on family news and to enjoy their company after years of communicating only by mail. By then Pepe had married. He and his wife, Carolina, were raising two children of their own, a boy and a girl. The girl, Carina, was four years old, exactly Remedios's age at the time of her accident. Spending time with the Riveras brought back many memories, including recollections of the other girl's accident back in May of 1971.

One afternoon, Pepe and I walked into town to observe the Semana Santa processions that take place in most Mexican towns. We stood on a sidewalk to watch processions of *penitentes* carry platforms bearing sacred images: Jesus dragging his cross to Calvary, Jesus crucified, Mary and Jesus in a *pietà*, Jesus in a glass coffin, Jesus risen as Christ Triumphant. At one point, when we stood before a church known locally as El Oratorio, Pepe motioned toward two young women standing across the street and off to the left. *"La Coica y Remedios,"* he told me. I did a double-take. La Coica, thirteen back in 1971, was now twenty-three or -four. Remedios, four years old when I last saw her, must have been sixteen now. Both were strikingly beautiful young women. The transformation of Remedios, especially, left me dumbstruck. Somewhat later, while walking through the town square, Pepe and I crossed paths with them again. This time we stood together on the sidewalk. I felt surprised by the warm smile that Remedios offered me. She shook my hand shyly and asked, *"¿Cómo le va?"* How amusing that she used the formal greeting! I asked her the same question, also in the formal. Nothing more. I felt moved to see her. A long, level pink scar crossed the center of her forehead: subtler than I would have expected, almost delicate. Our exchange arose and quickly ended. Once again I felt surprised, almost stunned, to sense a bond between us, some kind of pact that Remedios sealed with a lovely smile. The pang of protectiveness I felt toward her astonished me. The aftershock of responsibility? Her beauty, too, unnerved me. Why shouldn't a girl raised in small-town poverty blossom into a gorgeous young woman? Yet how easily the outcome might have been different. In the 1970's, Mexico's child-mortality rate remained appalling. Juan and Ángela Espinosa had lost five children. I felt gratified to discover that Remedios had reached young adulthood looking so healthy, fit, and lovely.

She and La Coica moved on.

On the way back to the house, Pepe and I ran into Rogelio. He was friendly but clearly drunk, and he looked awful—disheveled, haggard, almost elderly in appearance despite being only thirty-one or -two. He shook my hand over and over and wouldn't let go. *"¿Qué tal?"* I asked. *"Bueno, a veces bien y a veces mal,"* he answered, *"pero seguimos adelante, ¿no?"* Well, sometimes fine and sometimes bad, but we keep going forward, right?

Later, I asked Jesús and Alejandra about the Espinosas. Almost all of the family members, Alejandra told me, were doing pretty well. The girls continued to thrive. Most of the boys seemed to be managing, too, despite limited opportunities for employment in central Mexico.

"Antonio and Martín travel to Texas whenever they can," Jesús said. "That's the only place where they can find enough work to support the family."

"What about Rogelio?" I asked.

Alejandra answered in a grim, weary tone of voice: "Well, he takes after his father, so what can I say?" She made that tipping-of-the-bottle gesture with her right hand.

"And Juan?"

"He died somewhere in Texas," Jesús told me. "This happened four years ago. He was murdered—got shoved off a bridge." He spoke these words in a tone of resignation but without any drama, as if describing an ill-advised decision his brother had made.

Alejandra shook her head. "It's probably just as well for the family."

A FEW DAYS BEFORE I LEFT MEXICO, I climbed a ladder onto the concrete roof that Jesús and I, along with several of the Riveras' nephews and some of their neighbors, had poured before I'd left town in 1971. I gazed out at the panorama. The town dropped away below the Riveras' hillside property, then spread out to the right, to the left, and into the desert beyond. Only a few treetops obscured the lower reaches of this view. What mattered to me most just then was realizing that from my vantage, I could look straight down into the Espinosas' courtyard. Like many Mexicans' houses, theirs had a brick wall surrounding the living quarters and the patio. I felt as if I were peering into a tank. The interior lacked any vegetation or decoration; I saw only a packed dirt surface studded with rocks and littered with junk and trash. Nothing about this place looked appealing or safe. Most appalling was a rough-hewn ladder—two long, three-inch-thick saplings with lengths of scrap lumber nailed between them as rungs—resting diagonally against an unrailed second-floor balcony. This was the ladder that Remedios had fallen down. How could any parent have allowed a four-year-old to climb and descend such a dangerous setup? How could Juan and Ángela have put their kids in so much jeopardy? Perhaps they had no resources to do any better—not just financial resources but patience, forethought, and energy.

Remembering what I saw from that rooftop in 1983, I realize as I write this sentence now, almost five decades later, that since Remedios was four at the time of her accident, she must now be fifty or fifty-one years old. She is probably the mother of grown sons and daughters—indeed, she may well have grandchildren. Is she well? Is she happy? I'll never know. Jesús and Alejandra both died a long time ago. Despite my efforts to stay in touch, I've lost track of Pepe, Carolina, and their kids. If I traveled back to their town, I could visit the barrio, knock on doors, ask questions of the neighbors. I could—but I won't. Maybe it's best to leave well enough alone. Yet I can't resist hoping that Remedios has thrived over all these years; that her family has worked their way out of wretched poverty; and that her kids and grandkids have never suffered, and will never suffer, the ills that befell her as a girl.

Grieving the death of a favorite student in "Elegy for Jane," Theodore Roethke laments the lack of any traditional context for his bereavement: "I, with no rights in this matter, / Neither father nor lover." I, too, found myself caught in a "matter" like Roethke's. I had no rights. Even lacking rights, however, I chose to have responsibilities. Was that choice presumptuous?

Perhaps. Risky? No doubt. Yet the choice made sense, and as a result I gave something to the injured girl. What's clearest to me, however, is that whatever I may have given Remedios back in 1971, I owe her deep gratitude for what she gave me: an opportunity to glimpse a way of caring for other people without expectation of reciprocity or recompense, a glimpse that prompted my ten years of work in acute-care hospital settings and, later, many years of work as an emergency medical technician.

Camera Obscura

What intrigues me most about the old camera: there's film inside. The circular red window at the back, transparent and slightly smaller than a dime, shows the number 3. Someone many years ago—decades, even—had loaded the Brownie and may have taken at least two snapshots. Will any resulting images have lasted after all that time?

With a black bellows protruding like a dog's snout, the Brownie resembles a miniature of the big portrait cameras that I had watched my uncle Alex, a professional photographer, use many years ago. Everything about this device speaks of a bygone era. Even its odor, dusty and musty, reveals the passage of time. I had purchased it while visiting a rural antique store in Maine. How old is it? Unclear. NO. 2 FOLDING AUTOGRAPHIC BROWNIE reads the gold lettering underneath the lens assembly. My curiosity intensifies. I punch the name into a search engine and learn that Eastman Kodak manufactured this line of products between 1917 and 1926. If this one dates from the early years of that span, the camera is over a hundred years old. If from the later range, then just eight years shy of a century.

My curiosity intensifies. Can I get the film developed? I can't resist wondering what might appear. A family at a picnic, perhaps?—the men in linen suits and boater hats, the women in flapper outfits, the girls in frocked dresses, the boys in sailor suits. Or maybe two teenage sisters posing in an orchard? Or some ballplayers lined up for a team portrait? Or a newlywed couple standing nervously with their parents? These possibilities—any possibilities—entice me and draw me forth.

A dark thought occurs to me: whoever took the pictures, as well as the people "captured" on film, must now be either ancient or dead. Even a baby photographed in, say, 1920, will now be a man or a woman almost a hundred years old—assuming, of course, that he or she is still alive at all. The odds of such a long life are slim; even the subject of a baby photo has probably been dead for decades. Same for the older members of the picnic party, the sisters, the baseball players, the newlyweds. Anyone whose images I might find among the photos will most likely be long gone.

I visit a local camera store to inquire about getting the film developed. By raising this issue almost two full decades into the twenty-first century, I realize that my request is the equivalent of asking the personnel at an audio specialty store if they can repair the wax cylinders for a Victrola. I explain the situation to Bob, the owner: "Do you guys offer this kind of service for old film?"

Bob, gruff and busy, sounds skeptical about the likelihood of finding images on the old film. "Not very often," he tells me. "Almost nobody bothers to develop black-and-white film these days. Also, if there's anything present on really old film, the images will be of very poor quality."

Since he seems hesitant to proceed—more than hesitant: uninterested—I hold off. I take the camera home and put it away.

IN ENGLISH WE SAY "develop the film" or "get the film developed," and the equivalent phrase in other languages often relies on the same verb. The idiom in French is *développer une pellicule*—almost the same as in English. In Italian? *Svippulare il film*, once using again a verb that means "to develop." Similarly, the German phrase is *entwickle den film*, with an equivalent verb. Russian? развить фильм (*razvit' film*). Mandarin: *Kāifā diànyǐng*—developing a film. In Spanish, however, the relevant phrase is *revelar la película*—"to reveal the film." Spanish somehow describes the process most accurately, most vividly, the process that anyone witnesses when observing the alchemy of darkroom processes. This is what I want: not just development but *revelation*.

In many ways the lexical differences between languages don't matter much anymore. Few people nowadays take photos using film. Digital photography is the twenty-first-century norm. Development—revelation—is instantaneous. Where, then, does this leave me, with the antique camera sitting idle on my dresser, the film inside having been exposed at least sixty or seventy years ago, perhaps eighty or ninety, possibly a hundred?

I CONTACT A SPECIALTY PHOTO SERVICE in Kansas I've located online, I explain my situation, and I ask if the company might help me out. "I realize that the odds aren't great for a positive outcome," I write in my initial e-mail, "and perhaps for any outcome at all. Even so, I'm curious to see what's there. Would your company be able to develop the negatives and see if there's anything worth printing? Are you willing to give it a try?"

The response comes just a few hours later: "Yes, we process black and white 120 film. I've attached an order form for you to use. A lot of people send film that turns out. It just depends on where the film has been stored."

Without further delay I rewind the film inside the camera, remove the roll, wrap it in foil, package it, and mail it to Kansas.

I RECEIVE AN E-MAIL from the photo service eight days later, not a message as such but a refund for credit-card charges and a terse explanation for the refund: "Roll has no images." Despite this bad outcome, I'm still curious about the film. When I sent the roll to the photo service, I requested that they return it to me even if the darkroom process *revealed* nothing. A little package arrives a few days later. Inside the envelope are the company's receipt and paperwork, the film's metal spool with

a roll of paper still wound around it, plus a white paper pack-
et containing six five-inch-long strips of the film itself. All six
appear to be completely blank. Holding them up to the light,
all I can see is a delicate, nearly invisible pattern of striations
on the outer surface, not entirely a crazing of the acetate but
something similar—micro-wrinkles, perhaps, resulting from
degraded chemicals on the acetate. Otherwise nothing.

I'm disappointed, of course. No picnickers gaze back at me.
No sisters smile serenely in the orchard. No baseball players
pose together, all lined up and earnest, bats and mitts ready for
action. No newlyweds glance nervously at each other in their
parents' presence. Even a shadowy image would have been at
least one fish in the net I've cast. Instead, I've hauled it up altogether empty.

Or have I? Looking more closely at the strips of film, I see
one of them showing more than just the almost imperceptible
striations evident on the acetate. There's an oval smudge
present on the left-hand third of the strip. What am I seeing?
Perhaps nothing but some aberrations in the silver halide
crystals coating the film? Or maybe a thumbprint left there
by a lab technician at the Kansas photo service? I examine the
smudge more closely. With a jolt I realize that what I'm seeing
may not be a smudge after all. What, then? An image. Of what?
It's possible that despite the faintness of what I'm viewing—its
attributes bleached almost to non-existence—this oval may be
what remains of a human face.

Then I pull back not just from the film but from the notion
I've started to entertain. This is ridiculous. I am literally *imagining* the face. What I tell myself I'm seeing doesn't actually exist.
My perception is the equivalent of fervent Christians seeing
Jesus stare back at them from a piece of toast. Hungry and sug-
gestible, the mind wants what it wants. I crave an image somewhere in this roll of almost transparent acetate; hence an image
will arise. Like a child gazing at summer clouds in hopes of
spotting a unicorn or a whale, I will see what I want to see.

I put the strip away and ignore it for several days. Then, still curious, I take it out again, hold it up to the window and the overcast sky beyond, peer at it toward the desk lamp and its beige shade, angle it this way and that, examine it in every way possible. It's not clear to me that something's there. It's not clear to me that *nothing* is there. Am I seeing the last vestiges of a toddler propped up in her crib, of an elderly woman sitting in her parlor, of a father posing in his frock coat, of a young woman gazing toward the photographer with a come-hither smile? Is this strip of plastic somehow haunted by a barely perceptible ghost? Is the image the ghost of a ghost? Or is it my own mind that's haunted, full of wishes for connection with someone who has never even existed?

Art of Memory, Art of Forgetting

Like seventeenth-century Puritans examining their souls for signs of salvation or damnation, Boomers scrutinize their minds for symptoms of dementia. They fret about forgetting where they parked the car. They worry about missing long-scheduled appointments. They ponder the significance of misusing familiar words or not recalling them in the first place. They contemplate their sometimes vague states of mind and wonder if this lack of clarity is merely fatigue or perhaps something more substantial, a mist that's creeping into their minds and leaving them fogbound. What they hear and read about cognitive and memory issues among seniors only deepens their concerns. Dementia affects a greater and greater percentage of the population. The lifetime risk for developing Alzheimer's disease, the most common form of dementia, is over twenty percent for women and over ten percent for men. Although people younger than Baby Boomers may not worry about such issues during youth or midlife—may even mock fretting seniors—these members of younger generations will almost certainly start to worry as they grow older. Many surveys of Americans' greatest fears rank dementia first, ahead even of death itself. All this I know: as a Boomer myself, I've lived long enough by now to work through the stages that morph from indifference to concern to persistent worry.

MEANWHILE, PEOPLE I KNOW not only express similar concerns but sometimes show actual signs of cognitive dysfunction. Two or three long-time friends inform my wife and me that they're having more than ordinary lapses of memory, and each of them worries that a neurological disorder may lie at the root of worsening forgetfulness. Several older members of our social circle, all in their mid-seventies or early eighties, seem less and less able to recall recent conversations. A boyhood friend of mine learns that a benign brain tumor is systematically and irrevocably dismantling his short-term memory. Edith and I are alarmed and saddened by what these friends are experiencing now and by what they face in the years ahead. We're also unnerved to grasp that we ourselves won't necessarily avoid similar problems in the future.

DURING MY TWENTIES, I worked for six years on Seven West, the neurology-neurosurgery ward at a large public hospital in Denver, Colorado. This job, which involved assisting nurses in bedside care of sick and injured patients, brought me face to face with severe medical problems I had only heard about— brain tumors, spinal injuries, Parkinson's disease, multiple sclerosis, cerebral hemorrhages, ischemic strokes, and many less common maladies. The setting was stressful, the work strenuous, the panorama of human misery often appalling. Despite the demands of looking after grievously ill men and women, however, I found the ward fascinating and often revelatory. One of the most remarkable aspects of my years on Seven West was perceiving the delicacy of personhood: how small, even tiny changes to the body's biochemistry and physiology—diminishment of neurons' dopamine production, deterioration of the nerves' myelin sheaths, mutations of the brain's glial cells—could dismantle not only one's physical health but also one's personality, the specific attributes of being that we tend to regard as inherent and unchanging. Even subtle damage to cell structure or to neurotransmitters can limit motor function, warp perception, dismantle the intellect, and irrevocably alter the nature of who we assume ourselves to be. Patients with symptoms of dementia were among those most consistently affected by such changes. These often older men and women, along with patients of any age who had suffered concussions or other brain injuries, usually manifested memory loss. Experiences washed through their minds but quickly dispersed like foam on the seashore.

Typical of patients with memory loss was Ellis, who arrived on Seven West for a two-day assessment. Accompanied by his wife, Margie, the eighty-year-old farmer was polite and cooperative when I visited his room to do the standard admission interview. I began the process by asking Ellis his name and date of birth. He could answer the first question but not the second. Subsequent questions stumped him. He specified his residence as "on the farm" but couldn't explain where it was. When I inquired about his reason for visiting Denver, he wasn't sure and expressed surprise when I explained that he'd been admitted to Colorado General: "I thought this was a hotel."

"No, it's a hospital," I told him.

"Huh! Why am I in the hospital?"

Margie smiled weakly. "Tell Ed about your memory."

"Nothing's wrong with my memory."

"Maybe so," I responded, trying to be non-confrontational, "but the doctors will help you decide."

He nodded vaguely.

I asked him the other intake questions—about overall health history, past illnesses, past surgeries, and so forth—each of which elicited a vague answer or none at all. Margie filled in the gaps. The gaps were, in fact, most of the interview. Then I gave the couple some information about the ward, the hospital, and resources in the immediate area. Margie asked a few questions, listened to my brief answers, and thanked me. I left. Ten or fifteen minutes later, she accosted me in the hall. "I need to tell you something," she said earnestly. "What you saw isn't Ellis. This isn't who he is! My husband has run a huge farm out near the Kansas border ever since his twenties. He's been successful his whole life long. He's a respected member of our community and an elder at our church. I don't know what's happening to him, but what he told you just now—how he's acting—isn't *him*." The families of many other patients afflicted with dementing illnesses often made similar disclaimers. The person they had brought to the hospital, the person they'd known and loved for so long, was now different, diminished, and sometimes already gone.

Two days later I learned Ellis's diagnosis: Alzheimer's disease. This and many other patients' cognitive problems over the years of my hospital work deepened my respect for the brain's complexity, my appreciation for how well it functions routinely, and my dread about how drastically it can go awry.

DEMENTIA ISN'T JUST ONE DISEASE but, instead, a potential consequence of many different conditions. Strokes, genetic defects, mis-folded prion proteins, hydrocephalus, traumatic brain injury, Down's syndrome, Alzheimer's disease, and non-Alzheimer's conditions can all lead to dementia. Of these illnesses and conditions, Alzheimer's disease is the most common.[1] The statistics about dementia are appalling. Alzheimer's disease is now so prevalent among the elderly as to resemble a plague. Approximately 5.5 million Americans are currently living with the consequences of Alzheimer's-related dementia. Eighty-two percent of these people are age 75 or older; the incidence of this malady correlates with increased age. Women with Alzheimer's disease outnumber men with the same condition by two to one. (The causes for this disproportion aren't yet clear.) Other factors—level of education, socioeconomic status, history of smoking and alcohol use, long-term diet, level of prior health care, and ethnicity, among others—are contributing factors in overall incidence. In any case, the number of persons with Alzheimer's disease will increase rapidly as the Baby Boom generation ages. Any Boomer who reviews the data and contemplates the situation has ample reason to feel alarmed.[2]

~~ ~~ ~~

AS MY WIFE AND I CONSIDER THESE ISSUES, we wonder to what degree we too may face issues of dementia. We monitor shifts in mental clarity, we note slips of the tongue, and we examine incidents in which forgetfulness plays a part—misplacing keys, forgetting items on a shopping list, losing track of dates on the calendar. Do these glitches simply reflect the normal course of aging? Or are they signs of a potential problem? We tend to give ourselves the benefit of the doubt. We feel fine overall. Our physicians keep signaling all-clear following our annual exams. We function well in our day-to-day activities— work, hobbies, financial tasks, volunteer commitments, and social engagements. We see no signs of smoke; hence we assume there's no fire. Even so, it's hard not to lie awake at night dreading the future.

KEEPING A DIARY is, whatever else, an attempt to extract and retain experiences from the passage of time. I can't prevent the flow, I can't dam it, but I can throw out a line and reel in some fish swimming there to keep in my private aquarium. I sometimes visit the tank to view the creatures now captive. I started keeping a journal at age eighteen. More than fifty years have passed since then. Over time the denizens of this menagerie look more and more unfamiliar, more exotic, more bizarre. The creatures who gaze back at me through the glass are my own experiences, are myself, yet I often contemplate them with surprise and bafflement. Was I truly like that in the past? Did I really do what I relate in my entries? Did I believe what I claim to? Was I indeed so involved with, so hostile toward, so enraptured with, so confused by the people I describe in such meticulous detail? I can now read what I wrote years or decades ago, but I often don't remember the events themselves, events that must have felt immediate and important, even powerful, when they took place.

Diaries and journals are clearly a form of salvage, a means

of retaining what would otherwise be lost, but I also find them recurrent reminders of loss itself, of the sheer number and variety of experiences that have vanished downstream. Journals mockingly refute the notion that much can be saved at all. I remember my high school friend Craig, now long deceased, but I can't recall why I felt so angry toward him in 1969. I remember Katie, a delightful young woman I met on the train between Arequipa and Puno during my 1971 travels in Peru, yet I have no recollection of why, overruling my strong inclination at the time, I decided to proceed alone to Cuzco rather than joining Katie on her trip to Lake Titicaca. I remember ruling out continued graduate studies in 1979, but I don't recall the discussion with professors that prompted my disengagement from the program. Some of the once-brilliant landscapes of my own life are now shadowy or impenetrably dark. Revisiting entries I wrote about innumerable incidents day after day, month after month, year after year, I often find images surfacing into my awareness but without conjuring other images, other experiences, other states of emotion. There are exceptions; it's not as if I'm uniformly amnesic. But most of what I recall now is simply what I portrayed on the page many years ago. The inconsistency of what floats to the surface, as well as the relative paucity of what emerges from the depths, astonish and appall me. I can't even guess the percentage of what's now lost, the proportion is so huge. Not all, certainly, but most of my own life has already receded into darkness.

THROUGHOUT 2016 I wrestled with a tenacious depression. I have experienced chronic, low-grade melancholia for most of my life, a kind of background static that's annoying and distracting but not disruptive. The slump I experienced during 2016 and early 2017 was different, worse, and more intense. It expressed itself as low mood, low energy, difficulty sleeping, fatigue, irritability, and mental fogginess. When I rummaged through my mind to identify the causes, several were obvious. My writing career wasn't going well. I'd been coping with some health issues. My social circle appeared to be narrowing—in part because Edith and I had moved to Vermont six years earlier, in part because many friends had pulled away while struggling with their own health problems and career difficulties. Several close friends were seriously ill. In addition, I felt unnerved by aspects of my own aging. (As a friend put it recently, "How long can we Boomers keep describing ourselves as 'in late middle age?' Surely there's a point where we simply have to admit we're *old.*") The *coup de grace* to my mood was a realization that as I approached my sixty-seventh birthday, my age would align with my mother's at the point of her life when she suffered a series of cerebral hemorrhages that eventually killed her. Did this alignment mean that I, too, would suffer hemorrhagic strokes? No. Or that I, too, would die fourteen months later? No. But the aggregate of the circumstances affecting me, among them the burden of memories about my mother at the same life stage, weighed on me and dragged me down. I lost my sense of purpose. To some degree I lost my sense of self. While I continued to find deep satisfaction in my marriage, in living on our Vermont property, and in our artistic and social activities there, I felt adrift in other ways.

Edith was supportive during that difficult year, but at some point she began expressing concerns about my state of mind and my behavior. She commented now and then that I was irritable; that I acted tense; that I seemed overly obsessed with physical work, almost to the point of hyperactivity; that I wasn't sufficiently attentive during our conversations; and, perhaps most troubling, that I repeated myself frequently and sometimes forgot what we had discussed. A couple of arguments during late 2016 and in early 2017 prompted her to press these points even more strongly than earlier. During a visit to our daughter in Mexico City that winter, a conversation one morning had deteriorated into another squabble. I had gotten upset with Edith and our daughter, and I had summarily left the room. After I'd walked off, our daughter had asked Edith, "What was *that* all about?" I learned later that our son had also expressed frustrations with my moodiness. When Edith and I discussed these incidents later, I couldn't recall some of them. I apologized for my behavior, reminded her that I'd been feeling low for months, and asked for a little more time to figure out the situation. Edith remained supportive but seemed to continue believing that I was more than just routinely out of sorts.

MY INTUITIVE SENSE was that no physiological problem lay at the root of my state of mind and behavior. Rather, the source was psychological. Given my lifelong propensity for mild depression, the current situation was surely just a matter of degree. It was a reaction to specific, temporary issues. I would work my way through them; then my state of mind would improve. The other issues that Edith noted surely had similar sources. I've always tended to be crabby when tired. I've always been absent-minded. I didn't believe that my forgetfulness had grown notably worse than in the past. I've always had an inconsistent ability to recall events, interactions, conversations, and dates on the calendar. I'm particularly bad with numbers. Remembering a long sequence of steps also feels daunting. When I prepare to perform a task, I often make a list to avoid getting sidetracked or delayed. Was it reassuring that these problems have always plagued me—that a bad memory is my status quo? Or was this background cold comfort, since it means having fewer marbles to lose in the long run?

I found it difficult both to answer these questions and to grasp the answers' implications. I still didn't believe that I was undergoing major changes. At the same time, I couldn't dismiss my family's concerns out of hand. I believed, however, that I could explain these states of mind and behavior in ways other than cognitive decline. Irritability and moodiness have many sources. Why shouldn't I be irritable and moody when my longstanding career had deteriorated? Why shouldn't I act stressed and obsessed with external work when I was pushing hard to reboot my career? Why shouldn't I be forgetful and repetitive when I was sleeping poorly night after night? Why shouldn't I be anxious as I slid from late middle age toward geezerhood? Isn't depression a common side effect of difficult life-stage transitions? Isn't anxiety, too, a common co-symptom of depression? Isn't it predictable that inattentiveness in conversations might occur when the mind buzzes with distracting, anxious internal chatter? Here again I couldn't easily answer these questions. As I struggled with them, however, I felt sympathetic toward Edith's frustrations—it's not fun to be around someone who's restless, spacey, and unhappy—but I continued to believe that the issues were fundamentally a side effect of depressing.

WITHOUT ANY PROMPTING from anyone, however, I decided to ask our physician for his opinion. I would value his opinion on whether I had anything to worry about. So, using the "patient portal" on his clinic's website, I raised the issues. He responded a day or two later:

> In this situation we typically do a screening memory test in our office. However, this screening test is not very accurate in detecting subtle changes in memory in certain individuals, especially those with higher education and cognitive function. I would suggest that we refer you to see Dr. Black, one of our neurologists here in town. She does a VERY comprehensive memory evaluation that is far more accurate than the testing we could provide you here. If that meets with your approval let me know and we can arrange the referral.

I appreciated his support but felt uneasy about undergoing a full evaluation. Was I opening doors best left closed? Maybe so. I was tempted to leave well enough alone. Yet after considering the options, I decided to go ahead. I wanted to honor my family's concerns. I didn't want to sink into denial. Moreover, I had observed neurologists in action and respected their nuanced perceptions. I valued Dr. Starr's opinion that a neurological consultation would be the best approach. Getting evaluated would clarify what I was facing: either I'd get a clean bill of health, or else I'd identify an issue genuinely worth monitoring. Either outcome would be worthwhile. As it turned out, a close friend, herself a physician, expressed high regard for Dr. Black. A few days later I scheduled the soonest available appointment—several months hence, unfortunately, but now at least slotted into the calendar. Then came the difficult task of waiting.

MANY DECADES AGO, the Argentine writer Jorge Luis Borges published a story called *"Funes el memorioso."* This story has long been celebrated throughout the literary world, including in the United States, but its title is difficult to translate effectively into English. "Funes" is a surname: the tale's main character is Ireneo Funes. But *"el memorioso?"* In Spanish, *memorioso* means "with or pertaining to a very good memory." In English, the forced neologism "memorious" is at best awkward and at worst bizarre. The story itself portrays the word better than any translation. In *"Funes el memorioso,"* the narrator explains that during his youth, while visiting an Uruguayan town, he met a teenager named Ireneo Funes. This boy was unremarkable except for his ability to know the precise time of day whenever asked. The author's interactions with Funes are brief and unremarkable at that time. Three years pass. On returning to Ireneo's town, the narrator learns that the young man had recently been bucked off a half-broken horse and left hopelessly disabled. "I was told [that Funes] never moved from his cot, with his eyes fixed on the fig tree in the back or on a spiderweb. In the afternoons, he would let himself be brought out to the window. He carried his pride to the point of acting as if the blow that had felled him were beneficial."

He told me that before that rainy afternoon when the blue-gray horse threw him, he had been what all humans are: blind, deaf, addle-brained, and absent-minded. . . . For nineteen years he had lived as one in a dream: he looked without seeing, listened without hearing, forgetting everything, or almost everything. When he fell, he became unconscious; when he came to, the present was almost intolerable in its richness and sharpness, as were his most distant and trivial of memories. Somewhat later he learned he was paralyzed. The fact scarcely interested him. He reasoned (he felt) that his immobility was a minimum price to pay. Now his perception and his memory were infallible. [3]

The narrator soon perceives that Funes now lives in a state of continuous, total recollection. He remembers everything he sees, hears, reads, dreams, and imagines. He remembers everything he has ever remembered. He has become *memorioso*.

Funes remembered not only every leaf of every tree in every patch of forest, but every time he perceived or imagined that leaf. He resolved to reduce every one of his past days to some seventy thousand recollections, which he would then define by numbers. Two considerations dissuaded him: a realization that the task was interminable, and the realization that it was pointless. He saw that by the time he died he would still not have finished classifying all the memories of his childhood.

The narrator notes that "The crippled boy's capacity for recall and his obsession with endlessly reviewing the infinite catalogue of recollection are foolish, even preposterous, but they revealed a certain halting grandeur. They allow us to glimpse, or to infer, the dizzying world that Funes lived in."

Not only was it difficult for him to see that the gener-
ic symbol "dog" took in all the dissimilar individuals
of all shapes and sizes, it irritated him that the "dog"
of three-fourteen in the afternoon, seen in profile,
should be indicated by the same noun as the dog of
three-fifteen, seen frontally. His own face in the mir-
ror, his own hands, surprised him every time he saw
them. . . . I suspect . . . that he was not very good at
thinking. To think is to ignore (or forget) differences, to generalize, to abstract. In the teeming world of
Ireneo Funes there was nothing but particulars—and
they were virtually *immediate* particulars. [4]

As if prefiguring Oliver Sacks's strange, revelatory, often
moving essays about patients with neurological conditions,
"Funes el memorioso" portrays a man trapped in the spiderweb
of excessive memory. Borges didn't know when he wrote his
story in the 1930's that many years later, medical researchers
would define the specific, disturbing condition that afflicted
Ireneo Funes. Hyperthymesia is a neurological disorder char-
acterized by detailed, even total recall of one's personal past.
People with hyperthymesia remember an abnormally vast
array of their life experiences. First categorized as a disorder
in 2006, hyperthymesia has two defining characteristics: first,
compulsive and excessive autobiographical recall; and second,
an extraordinary ability to remember specific events. ("Hyperthymesia" derives from two ancient Greek words: *hyper*
("excessive") and *thymesis* ("recollection"). This is a rare but remarkable condition. People experiencing hyperthymesia can
recall most or all days of their lives in meticulous detail; they
may also recall external events that have personal significance;
and these recollections arise without conscious effort. While
such abilities may sound positive, they are often disruptive.
Even people who are most aware and perhaps proud of their
capacity for hyper-memory—what we might call memorious-
ness—sometimes describe their condition in negative terms.

One patient has described her vast powers of recollection in these words: "Most have called [hyperthymesia] a gift but I call it a burden." She describes getting lost in her memories, which makes attending to the present difficult or impossible. "Whenever I see a date flash on the television (or anywhere else for that matter)," she states in an article about her condition, "I automatically go back to that day and remember where I was, what I was doing, what day it fell on and on and on and on and on. It is non-stop, uncontrollable and totally exhausting. I run my entire life through my head every day and it drives me crazy!!!"[5]

In some respects, hyperthymesia is the opposite of dementia. The demented man or woman experiences a crippling loss of memory. The person with hyperthymesia experiences a crippling overabundance of memory. Forgetfulness is a troubling, even alarming aspect of life for most people, but in some respects we need it. We lose thousands of perceptions, thoughts, sensations, emotions, and bits of information each day. We can't function effectively without this recurrent loss. We can't focus on the present if we find ourselves tangled in an intricate, sticky web of past experiences. Research into human neurological function reveals that the brain constantly, systematically erases memories. Several phases of sleep, for instance, serve (among other purposes) to remove as well as to consolidate memories. Like a computer emptying its cache and reorganizing data, the brain cleans up its hard drive. William James, writing in 1890, over a century before the advent of twenty-first-century neuroscience, summarized the issue succinctly: The "peculiar mixture of forgetting with our remembering is the very keel on which our mental ship is built. . . . If we remembered everything, we should on most occasions be as ill off as if we remembered nothing." [6]

Dementia traps you in the empty, boundless desert of forgetfulness. Hyperthymesia leaves you wandering through the overgrown jungle of remembrance. Either way you're lost.

❧ ❧ ❧

THE SPRING OF 2017 bloomed, thrived, and then matured into summer. Edith and I went about our work and our various projects. Although anxious about my upcoming July appointment with Dr. Black, I felt better in some respects. Getting past my early-April birthday allowed me to shed the anxiety I'd felt about its alignment with my mother's strokes at the same age. I moved on. My energy rebounded. I started sleeping better, eating better, getting more exercise, socializing more, and writing new books. My mood blossomed into something vibrant.

IN CONVERSATIONS ABOUT MEMORY and memory-loss issues, Boomers often advise and cajole one another. Sleep seven to eight hours each night. Get regular exercise. Drink alcoholic beverages just moderately or not at all. Eat cold-water fatty fish twice a week. Avoid refined sugar, processed foods, red meat, high-fat foods. Seek social and emotional support. Engage in mentally stimulating activities. All of these are standard-issue recommendations, none of which I dismiss and some of which I follow. Even so, I've grown weary of hearing them, a litany of sorts chanted by my aging peers in hopes of propitiating the god of memory. Specific bits of advice are even more tedious. Take 2,000 units of vitamin D. Take 500 micrograms of B-12. Take fish-oil supplements. Eat lots of kale. Drink green tea. Do crossword puzzles and Sudoku. Play Bananagrams and Scrabble. These last two morsels of advice I find particularly hard to swallow. Games and puzzles? I've always hated them. They bore me. They annoy me. Down deep I suspect that they don't so much prevent dementia as *cause* it. I'll just take my chances.

AN IDEA FOR THIS ESSAY came to me as I settled into bed one night, but by morning I couldn't remember what had occurred to me. Like a computer app crashing, my memory went blank. Was this a result of ordinary forgetfulness? Of something more ominous? I've always had a slipshod memory. Even as a boy I struggled with classroom tasks that required rote memorization. Multiplication tables, names of U.S. presidents, song lyrics, historical dates—these and most other facts and figures challenged my recall. Even memorizing Longfellow's "Psalm of Life," a sing-songy poem that my seventh-grade English teacher assigned to our class, took me weeks of struggle to accomplish. Later, during high school and college, I dreaded any class whose discipline rested on a bedrock of detailed information. Biology? An ordeal—all those genera and phyla. Chemistry? A nightmare of elements, atomic numbers, chemical properties, and periodic trends. Mathematics? Hopeless. My chosen studies of literature, languages, and psychology presented their own difficulties, but I found the challenges more manageable, given my verbal tendencies and interests. Even so, I often felt defeated by the effort required to stock my mind with names of authors, titles of their works, specific languages' tenses, declensions, and vocabularies, and the huge variety of concepts, and other data crucial for creative work in the humanities. Still later, as I established my career as a writer, I had to devise methods for recalling ideas, insights, and information necessary to write productively.

One method I used was scribbling notes whenever ideas came to me. Starting around 1968, I began keeping a small notebook in my back pocket. I also wrote longer entries in a larger journal. The smaller pad contained immediate observations, sensory perceptions, conjectures, questions, and ideas that floated through my mind—ephemeral thoughts that would otherwise rise up from the depths like bubbles, reach the surface, burst, and disappear. The larger notebook served as a more spacious place where the spontaneous jottings might expand. Most of what I wrote down served no purpose. I might easily have let these insights and perceptions vanish. A small number—two, three, five percent—seemed more durable. Over a period of time I found that even this small percentage justified scribbling the larger but less useful mass. What I saved became the component parts for a poem, a story, an essay, or even a novel. I would otherwise have attempted to build a house without stockpiling materials first—boards, nails, bricks, mortar, beams, rafters. People who saw me scribbling surely regarded me as eccentric or compulsive. Even friends sometimes mocked my habit of note-taking, and perhaps rightly so. I joined in the mockery, nicknaming the small notepads "my paper brain." At the same time, the method I devised proved useful and led to my writing and publishing dozens of books. It was also a stay of execution from the firing squad of forgetfulness.

So why, then, did I forget my essay idea that night? Because I often forget things. More so than in the past? Probably. Is the increased frequency a problem? Maybe, maybe not.

THE DAY OF MY NEUROLOGY APPOINTMENT arrived in mid-July. I went to the medical center feeling more anxious than I'd expected. The magnitude of this evaluation wouldn't rank with, say, discussing biopsy results for an excised tumor, yet I grasped how fully the outcome might change the path ahead. What if Dr. Black told me, "Well, I do see some evidence of cognitive changes"? Or: "Tests indicate what we call mild cognitive impairment." Or, worse yet, "Unfortunately, we can't quite rule out early-stage Alzheimer's." While these outcomes didn't seem likely, they weren't impossible. For this reason, I waited in the reception area feeling uneasy and tense.

Once I met Dr. Black in her examination room, however, she put me more at ease. She was cordial, poised, and inquisitive from the start. Mid-sixties in age, lean, and dark-haired, she met my gaze with her clear blue eyes. She had a high voice and a clear, calm style of communication. We started our discussion by commenting about the mutual friend who is a physician at the same medical center and who shares our interest in classical music.

Soon we shifted to the medical topic at hand. Dr. Black started by asking a series of questions about why I'd sought her medical insights and advice. What was my overall state of health? What difficulties had I experienced that might suggest a neurological or cognitive condition? Specifically, what might imply memory issues? I explained that I didn't necessarily believe I had a problem—at least not beyond the occasional, specific, pesky memory lapses that almost everyone starts to experience in late midlife; however, my family had expressed concerns that I couldn't dismiss and that I needed and wanted to respect. Dr. Black and I discussed the situation further. Then, after asking about my family's health history and other background issues, she performed the neurological exam. I knew from my hospital job back in the 1970's that the neuro exam is a sensitive tool for identifying many issues. Dr. Black asked me to perform several different motions: moving my eyes, sticking out my tongue, touching the tip of my nose with my index finger, and so forth. She tested my hearing and sense of smell. She had me identify the numbers she traced with her fingertip on the palm of my hand. She tested my reflexes. Then, after asking further questions to assess cognition and memory, she said, "Your neurological test is normal. I don't detect any deficits at all." I was pleased, of course, to hear this assessment. She continued: "However, we have a battery of tests that would give us a more nuanced picture. They focus specifically on memory issues and provide much more data to work from." She asked if I wanted to take these tests, which would require ninety minutes of my time.

At first I felt reluctant. Why ask for trouble when I apparently found myself in the clear? Why go looking under rocks? Why risk finding some awful snake lurking there? But I decided to proceed anyway. Since Dr. Black's initial assessment was positive, the risk of a bad outcome now seemed lower than before. If the test indicated a problem, however, I felt I'd rather know than not know.

Dr. Black alerted one of her assistants, who led me to a separate room and set me up for the tests. A computer terminal with a special keyboard rested on a countertop. Once the assistant left, I worked my way through the sequence. Each of nine or ten tests showed objects on the monitor or asked brief written questions, each of which required a quick response on the keyboard. Later, I learned that these tests monitor fine-motor control, speed of response, visual memory, speed of data processing, retention of information, ability to stay focused, ability to interpret emotions (as manifested by facial expressions in photographs), and accuracy in perceiving visual and abstract information. I found the tests repetitive, tedious, and sometimes exasperating. One of the most daunting involved observing colored shapes—triangles, circles, squares—that the screen presented in rapid succession. Accurate response required noting when a certain shape had appeared not one but two shapes past. This and other tasks started out easy but grew more and more complex. I often felt frustrated when attempting to respond. I started to worry about my performance. Finishing the battery, I believed that my scores would be so low as to indicate a problem after all. I felt anxious, deflated, and concerned.

WHAT DOES IT MEAN to have "a normal memory"? For most people, this means remembering well enough to function in the day-to-day world. I seem to fall comfortably into this category. I wake up recalling what activities and relationships need my attention. I remember what day it is. I recall the information necessary to perform business tasks and domestic duties: phone numbers, appointments, errands, household chores. I remember the current status of my work and what I should do next. In the context of my marriage and friendships, I generally recall whatever needs a response—promises to keep, questions to answer, help to offer, birthdays and anniversaries to remember. I successfully find my way through time and space by means of adequate recall. I generally know where I left my keys and where I've parked the car. Is this jumble of recollections sufficient? Probably.

Even so, these aspects of memory, though important, are *only* normal. They are literally the *norm.* Yet memory can go far beyond the quotidian aspects of getting through the days, weeks, months, and years. Each of us has ways in which our faculties of memory are comparatively strong or comparatively weak. A high school friend possessed an almost Aspergerian capacity for absorbing scientific data, including his ability to memorize the entire periodic table by age fifteen: not just the names of all the elements but also their atomic numbers, atomic weights, groups, periods, and categories. More recently, another friend taught herself to play and then committed to memory all twenty-four of the intricate, difficult preludes and fugues from Book One of J.S. Bach's *Well-Tempered Clavier.* A man I read about, a professional linguist with no knowledge of Finnish, studied a grammar and a lexicon for that language during an overnight flight from New York to Helsinki; he memorized the grammatical rules and much of the vocabulary; and, following his nocturnal cram-course, he arrived at his destination able to converse articulately among the Finns. My wife and I were astonished to realize during our son's childhood that he possessed eidetic memory—often called "photographic memory"—which allowed him even at age eight or nine to read technical computer coding manuals before bedtime, sleep through the night, go to school the next day, and then practice website design after school "by reading the pages I saw in my head," as he described the situation. (Eidetic memory is rare, present mostly in children between the ages of six and twelve. Following that stage of development, most persons possessing eidetic memory lose that heightened capacity for recalling images and information.[7])

More daunting still is the fact that in ancient Greece, ancient Rome, and Renaissance Europe, rhetoricians and scholars developed *ars memoriae,* the Art of Memory, a set of disciplines that allowed practitioners to mentally archive vast quantities of knowledge. The Art of Memory used techniques that would strike many people in our own era as bizarre, daunting, and laborious. Our modern habit, modus, and first recourse is easy access to printed and digital resources. (As a friend stated recently, "Why should I remember *anything* when I can look up *everything?*") One common technique among the ancient practices was the so-called "memory palace," a mnemonic system that involved imagining a huge architectural structure—a house, theater, or temple—in which the practitioner then stockpiled individual rooms with subcategories of the information that he or she wished to recall. Possibly invented by the Greek poet Simonides of Ceos (556-468 BCE) and modified during subsequent eras, this and similar systems allowed people to memorize long speeches, bodies of knowledge (rhetoric, science, theology), and epic poems.[7] In the pre-literate age, educated people relied on memorizing information, a reliance that progressively strengthened the faculty of memory from childhood on. The advent of reading in the ancient Europe, followed by the growing availability of books during the European Renaissance, reduced the appeal of mnemonic systems. As Plato predicted in *The Republic,* the rise of reading would foster the decline of memory.[8] (We can only begin to imagine Plato's opinion of the Internet, of digital apps, and of all the twenty-first century gadgets that encourage us to abandon our own cognitive skills and rely on technology instead.)

All of the abilities I've described here seem beyond my reach. I've never been able to recall more than a few bits of information from the periodic table. I have no talent for memorizing music. I've forgotten almost all of the various languages I've studied over the years and even some of the Spanish I learned as a child and have spoken my whole life long. I have only a basic capacity to recall visual images and none for reading pages conjured in my mind. With these and my many other inabilities, non-talents, incapacities, and limitations, am I normal or deficient?

I RETURNED TO DR. BLACK'S EXAMINATION ROOM ready to hear bad news.

When Dr. Black entered and settled in again, now holding the printout of my test results, she said, "I see nothing at all that would prompt any concern. There's nothing in your results that suggests any kind of dementia or precursor to dementia. The cognitive and memory tests are all normal. Brain function by domain is fine. Memory is normal and intact."

It's hard for me to overstate the relief I felt.

Dr. Black handed me a copy of the printout and explained the findings. "You're well within normal limits on all the tests," she said. "You're either within or above the standard percentile. Symbol Digit Coding is the most sensitive test, and you did fine on that. You did fine on different aspects of the Continuous Performance Test." She worked her way through the list. "You did less well on the Emotional Recognition Test"—which asks the patient to identify the emotions shown in a series of facial photographs—"but, frankly, this is not a good test." Dr. Black agreed with me when I commented that the emotions displayed on the faces were ambiguous, hence potentially frustrating. She assured me that my average score on the Emotional Recognition Test didn't indicate a problem.

What about the issues I'd raised earlier—including the issues prompting family members' concerns over the past year? What about my irritability, my occasional memory lapses, and my depression? "What you describe is routine for your stage of life. These are very common issues as people age," Dr. Black told me, "and they can cause false alarms about cognitive issues. These are transient. They aren't precursors to dementia. The issues that cause the most frequent false alarms are pain, sleep deprivation, anxiety, depression, and various medications." She made it clear that my life-stage issues, rather than neurological problems, were the source of my difficulties. She predicted that they would pass.

I found one of Dr. Black's final comments especially reassuring. When I commented on some aspect of my work as a novelist and essayist, she asked, "Are you still writing?"

"A lot. New things—quite a few."

"Good!" she told me. "Because if you really were having any issues with dementia, your writing would be the first thing to go."

Dr. Black's final remarks: "Take the report home, put it away, and don't even think about it. You're fine. If you have concerns in the future, call me. We now have a baseline to work from."

Did her upbeat assessment surprise me? Not really. It was consistent with my intuitions. Did I feel relieved anyway? Of course—intensely so. Intuition has its merits, but confirming intuition with empirical data and with a doctor's expert perceptions is even better. On returning home, I described the exam, the testing, and the final discussion to Edith. She too was jubilant. Each of us felt as thrilled as we have in the past when we've received diagnostic reports indicating that a suspected malignancy was benign after all.

DOES THIS OUTCOME mean I'm in the clear? Does it prove that I've avoided the Dark Wood of forgetfulness? Perhaps for now, but not forever. To quote a statement that the environmentalist David Brower once wrote in a different context: "Our victories are temporary but our losses are permanent." Although I'm free of memory problems in my late sixties, I have no guarantee that I won't stray into the forest at seventy-five, eighty, or later. Some factors work in my favor—overall good health, no history of smoking or heavy drinking, a healthful diet, and, so far as I can tell, good genes. But who knows? Even if I retain good cognition and live to a hundred, death itself is inevitable, and with death will come the full erasure of my memory. When I remark on this fact to friends, most say, *Don't be so depressing!* What's the benefit, however, of denying reality? No extra doses of vitamins D or B_{12}, no additional salmon dinners, no hyperintense workouts on the elliptical, no upgraded program of crossword puzzles, Sudoku, Scrabble, or other memory games will spare me from eventual extinction.

IRENEO FUNES WAS *MEMORIOSO*—flooded with memories. We might call the opposite of this state being *olvidadizo*, a Spanish word that somehow hits harder than the English equivalent, "forgetful." Normal aging includes the diminishment of memory. This is a disturbing process but also inconvenient, frustrating, worrisome, exasperating, embarrassing. Unfortunately, a weakening of the memory is almost inevitable. Like reductions in energy, falling out of hair, disruption of sleep, wrinkling of skin, and all the other losses that accompany advancing years, we have to face the diminishment of memory rather than pretending we'll somehow circumvent this aspect of life.

I'M AMAZED, MEANWHILE, almost overwhelmed, by how much I still remember. Memory isn't just a Dark Wood, it's also a lush rainforest. Each day I find myself hacking a path through the intricate thickets of memory. Some of what I recall pertains to quotidian tasks: groceries to buy, messages to write, appointments to keep, bills to pay, chores to do. Some recollections connect one sense impression to another: a flicker's cry in the Vermont woods vividly evokes a flicker in my family's backyard sixty years ago. A friend's random comment about Machu Picchu suddenly prompts me to remember the list of Inca rulers I'd memorized (*Manco Capac, Inca Roca, Tupaq Yupanqui* . . .) while living in Lima as a ten-year-old. I shove my way into and past this underbrush all day long. Is it reassuring to have all this mental vegetation to push through? Perhaps—both to have the forest around me and to know there's a way out. But it's true that remembrance of things past often sharpens even as—or perhaps because— short-term recall grows dull. Maybe the lushness is a sign of aging. And as we age, it's possible to get lost in the labyrinth of what's now long gone. I find it consoling, however, that my memory remains sharp for the most important events of my life. I recall the details of crossing paths with Edith at Gatwick Airport in 1979, a chance encounter that led to our courtship for several years, our wedding in 1985, and our marriage ever since. I clearly remember the births of our two children: our daughter's routine delivery, attended by midwives; and our son's sudden, premature arrival at the end of Edith's difficult second pregnancy. I recall what seems a kaleidoscopic sequence of events from our years as a family. I remember what seems a limitless number of interactions with friends, acquaintances, co-workers, and total strangers over a period of almost seven decades. I recall, too, much of my progress through my life's *jardín de senderos que se bifurcan,* as Borges called it—the garden of forking paths. So complex is the path for each of us that it's no wonder we can't recall the whole network and what happened along the way. Unless we are blessed with (or cursed by) hyperthymesia, we will inevitably forget most of what we've experienced.

Is it possible that what we're striving for isn't *ars memoriae* so much as *ars obliviosi*? Not the Art of Memory but the Art of Forgetfulness? Not the art of amassing great stores of information but, rather, the art of graciously letting that stockpile diminish?

IN ANCIENT GREEK MYTHOLOGY, Lethe was the river of forgetfulness. The shades of the dead, descending into Hades, drank from Lethe's flowing waters and lost all memory of their earthly life. "Of this [river] they were all obliged to drink a certain quantity," Plato has Socrates state in Book Ten of *The Republic.* "[E]ach one as he drank forgot all things." [9] Death wipes clean the memory because it wipes out everything. More alarming still is the possibility that life itself is the River Lethe: that for most people who live long enough, drinking from the flow of years will erase recollections—maybe all recollections—of one's time on earth. If so, perhaps just by living long enough we're all drinking from the River Lethe.

It's difficult not to find this prospect unnerving, alarming, even terrifying.

In the meantime, however, I experience each day, and I delight in each day, fully confident that although life may be Lethe (or perhaps just lethal) for the time being its swift current remains full, complex, rich, and invigorating, health howsoever long or brief.

Don't Jump!

et's suppose that astronomers detect a previously unnoticed asteroid somewhere out there in the solar system. Initial projections of this space rock's orbit prompt some concern. NASA, the European Space Agency, and other organizations analyze the preliminary data and collectively reach an appalling conclusion: the object in question is huge—hundreds of meters in diameter—and its path around the sun places it on a collision course with our planet. Calculations indicate that the asteroid will crash into Earth on March 3rd five years hence. The size of the rock all but guarantees massive damage to the global environment—widespread flooding of coastal areas, violent disruption of the atmosphere, years of severe weather events, dramatic reductions in the worldwide food supply, famine in some regions, and other calamities that will put all nations' economies under severe strain, prompt especially acute suffering in less-affluent countries, spark local, regional, and international conflicts as resources diminish, and cause millions of human deaths and the extinction of countless non-human species in the longer term.

The initial reaction to this news is widespread panic. Soon, however, a more thoughtful, more organized response takes shape. Early discussions within the scientific community lead to an international conference that focuses on verifying the data, outlining approaches to address the threat, and mobilizing resources to solve the problem. More than a hundred nations participate. Although some outbreaks of squabbling, posturing, and one-upmanship erupt, those reactions occur less often than most observers would have expected. The situation becomes the global equivalent of Samuel Johnson's famous dictum that "when a man knows he is to be hanged in a fortnight, it concentrates his mind wonderfully." A consensus develops with surprising speed: the most technologically advanced nations must intervene on behalf of the entire planet. NASA, the European Space Agency, the China National Space Agency, the Russian State Corporation for Space Activities, and other governmental entities will collaborate with private-sector companies in several dozen countries to mount an anti-asteroid space program. This consortium will build a specially outfitted spacecraft, launch it with four astronauts on board, rendezvous with the space rock ten months later, deflect it onto a harmless trajectory, disengage, and then return (if possible) to earth. Ambitious? Indeed—more so than any space mission ever attempted. But neglecting to make the attempt will doom everyone on earth to unimaginable suffering. There's no sensible alternative.

What most observers find remarkable as the crisis evolves is both the degree and the speed of agreement about this plan. Most people in most countries support it. Is this relative harmony so remarkable? Not at all. The threat is clear-cut. The consequences of inaction are appalling. The proposed solution isn't perfect, but it's technically attainable. The economic sacrifices required are acceptable. Despite the long, squalid history of human discord, most citizens throughout the world, as well as most of their leaders, agree that this difficult mission must proceed. The overwhelming majority of human beings put aside their political, ethnic, religious, and national differences and strive to collaborate. Perhaps inevitably, various fringe groups object to the mission: a small minority of Christian fundamentalists view the asteroid as a righteous expression of God's wrath; a scattering of Muslim extremists decry the mission as an affront to Allah's will; a few Hindu radicals claim that the space rock's heralds the onset of the Kali Yuga; and a variety of freelance fanatics object for other reasons. Yet most people believe that intervention is the only sensible response to the calamities that will otherwise commence in just a few years.

The fantasy I've sketched here won't take place. (At least not in the immediate future. A recent NASA survey, however, lists 4,700 space rocks large enough to pose a significant danger to life on earth, and others may be out there as yet undetected.[1]) If a scenario like this one arose, would the world's nations collaborate to eliminate the threat? It's possible that my notion of international collaboration is too optimistic. I believe, however, that an imaginative response to the menace of a "doomsday rock" would be more probable than not. In any case, focused collaboration seems likelier than the alternate scenario: that the wealthiest, most technologically advanced nation on earth would drag its heels, attempt to shove the problem under the carpet, and pretend that everything will be just fine if we simply ignore the abundant scientific data confirming the danger. Nor is it likely that prominent American executives would invest millions of dollars from their corporate and personal coffers to fund disinformation campaigns about the asteroid's impending arrival. Think tanks wouldn't hold international conferences to debunk "space rock alarmists." Nor would swarms of lobbyists descend daily on Capitol Hill to pressure lawmakers against funding the anti-asteroid space program. Members of Congress, like their rich corporate donors and everyone else, would grasp that their own lives, as well as the lives of their children and grandchildren, will be in grave peril if they ignore the calamity drawing closer with each passing day. They would take action to save themselves, their families, their communities, and the wider world.

∽ ∽ ∽

"It's not something dramatic now—that's why people don't really react."

—H. Jay Zwally, Ph.D., NASA scientist [2]

WHY ISN'T THE EQUIVALENT TAKING PLACE now regarding global climate disruption? Research shows a continuing accumulation of greenhouse gases in the atmosphere and a resultant steady, unprecedented rise in global temperatures. While it's true that no one fully understands yet how these changes will affect the earth, it's almost certain that the consequences will be dire. The global climate is changing rapidly. Alarming, intensifying consequences are already evident worldwide. The Arctic ice is shrinking. The Greenland ice sheet is melting. Glaciers worldwide are retreating. Massive icebergs—recently, one the size of Connecticut—are breaking free from Antarctica. Drought is afflicting Australia, the American Southwest, California, China, sub-Saharan Africa, the Indian subcontinent, and the Amazonian basin. Wildfires are growing more frequent, more intense, and more destructive in many parts of the world. The oceans are warming and turning acidic. The Siberian permafrost is melting, releasing millions of tons of heat-trapping methane each year.

Why, then, are so many people intent on ignoring the problem of climate disruption? One reason is cognitive dissonance. How can we, who are so thoughtful, so well intentioned, so *wonderful*, be complicit in causing such a terrible a problem? Another is ordinary wishful thinking. Another is a massive failure of imagination. Still another the uncertainty over how and when the chickens will come home to roost. Unlike the scenario of an earth-bound asteroid, climate disruption won't occur precisely on March 3rd in a specific year. The hangover from our drunken binge on oil won't hit us all at once. How much easier, then, to keep on guzzling the petrochemical brew we love so much.

Ironically, it's conservatives—some of whom are climate-change deniers—who have offered a parable that fits the situation perfectly. Over the past several decades, I've heard many Right-leaning Americans invoke an old folk tale: How to Boil a Frog. The recipe? Start by putting several inches of cold water into a kettle. Sick a frog in the water. The frog will stay put because he feels comfortable there. Then turn on the burner to a low flame. If you toss a frog into boiling water, he'll hop right out; with a gradual warming, however, he'll just sit there. By keeping the heat gentle but steady, you'll prevent the frog from grasping what's about to happen. He won't even sense the change. By the time he notices the water is hot enough to cook him, he's too late to take action.

Conservatives often invoke this parable to warn about the dangers they fear—creeping socialism, encroaching immigration, erosion of gun rights, and so forth. Yet How to Boil a Frog is also particularly appropriate regarding human beings' inability to perceive and acknowledge global climate change. The steady rise of CO_2 levels in the atmosphere and the resulting steady rise of temperatures are easy to ignore and tempting to explain away. Conservative candidates routinely dismissed climate-change science during the 2016 presidential campaign. Donald Trump notably mocked concerns about climate issues ("It's really cold outside. . . . Man, we could use a big fat dose of global warming!"). Many state- and local-level Republicans have neglected or dismissed the problem as well. Following Trump's inauguration in January of 2017, the new president moved quickly to undo the modest efforts that President Obama had made to counter climate change. The Trump administration withdrew the United States from the Paris Agreement to limit greenhouse gas emissions; the Environmental Protection Agency moved quickly to reverse regulatory efforts affecting the environment, including climate disruption; and the administration has clearly allied itself with corporate interests, including the fossil-fuel industries, on almost all environmental issues.

❧   ❧   ❧

"It may seem impossible that a technologically advanced society could choose, in essence, to destroy itself, but that is what we are now in the process of doing."

—Elizabeth Kolbert [3]

THE CUMULATIVE SCIENTIFIC DATA indicate that we humans
are rapidly changing the global ecosystems that have been
hospitable to our species, and to the species we depend upon,
for many thousands of years. Global climate change is only
the most widespread and drastic sign of the damages that we
Homo sapiens are inflicting. Destruction of forests, acidification
of the oceans, desertification of the land, depletion of aquifers,
extinction of species, pollution of the atmosphere—the list goes
on and on in showing the numerous, extensive ways in which
we are despoiling our planet. The damage may take decades to
play out, but the harm is progressive, it's increasing in quantity
and severity, it appears to be accelerating, and it may well
be irreversible. Our species may be the collective equivalent
of someone perched on a tall building and ready to leap. Or
we have already made the leap itself but simply haven't hit
bottom yet.

When I raise concerns about ecological crises with friends
and acquaintances, many people express their own anxieties.
My home state, Vermont, is "green" in many ways and has a
relatively good track record on environmental issues. Many
people I know here share my worries about climate disruption
and other threats to the global environment. Others, however,
seem skeptical. I often hear expressions of doubt, even of
derision. "Oh, I don't think global warming is such a big deal,"
one local farmer tells me. "We've always had ups and downs
in seasonal temperatures. Those are just part of the natural
cycle." Another neighbor says, "Those environmentalists are
making a mountain out of a mole hill." Another, commenting
on a recent cold snap, jokes, "Where's global warming when
we need it!" Yet another, incensed when I simply mention the
issue of climate disruption, exclaims: "Global warming is a
hoax!"

Yet cognitive dissonance and denial aren't the only source
of people's disbelief. In addition, some organizations have

made concerted efforts to spread misinformation about climate disruption. Notable among them is the Heartland Institute, based in Arlington Heights, Illinois. As this group's website states, "The mission of The Heartland Institute is to discover, develop, and promote free-market solutions to social and economic problems" including "market-based approaches to environmental protection . . . " These "market-based approaches" include an emphasis on supporting the fossil-fuel industry and attempting to counter environmental scientists' concerns about global climate disruption. The Heartland Institute has hosted ten "International Conferences on Climate Change" intended to cast doubt on the theory that human actions cause global warming, a theory that the Institute labels "climate alarmism." Heartland has, in fact, "conducted a comprehensive communications and marketing campaign . . . to confront 'junk science.'" (The Heartland Institute's definition of "junk science" appears to be any research that presents fossil fuels as the primary cause of global climate change.) This organization sells books with titles like *Nothing to Fear: A Bright Future for Fossil Fuels* and *Why Scientists Disagree about Global Warming*.[4] The Heartland Institute also places paid advertisements on Google and other sites so that any search for "global warming" or "climate change" will give top billing to their climate-change-denial website, publications, and press releases.

If these efforts and the ideas they promote had independent origins—if they resulted from individuals' skepticism about climate change—their conclusions would still be questionable. The massive evidence that climate change has human origins becomes more difficult to refute with each passing year. What makes The Heartland Institute's activities and policies even more problematic is the clear connection between this organization and the fossil fuel industry. The same holds true for other climate change-denying "think tanks." As Naomi Klein writes in *This Changes Everything: Capitalism vs. The Climate*, her detailed commentary on the climate crisis, "The deniers are doing more than protecting their personal worldviews—they are protecting powerful political and economic interests that have gained tremendously from the way Heartland and others have clouded the climate debate." She goes on to write:

> The ties between the deniers and those interests are well known and well documented. Heartland has received more than $1 million from ExxonMobil together with foundations linked to the Koch brothers and the late conservative funder Richard Mellon Scaife. Just how much money the think tank receives from companies, foundations, and individuals linked to the fossil fuel industry remains unclear because Heartland does not publish the names of its donors . . . Indeed, leaked internal documents revealed that one of heartland's largest donors is anonymous—a shadowy individual who is given more than $8.6 million specifically to support the think tank's attacks on climate science.[5]

Klein notes as well that The Heartland Institute isn't alone in its close ties to the fossil fuel industry.

> [S]cientists who present at Heartland climate conferences are almost all so steeped in fossil fuel dollars that you can practically smell the fumes. To cite just two examples, the Cato Institute's Patrick Michaels, who gave the 2011 conference keynote, once told CNN that 40% of his consulting companies income comes from oil companies (Cato itself has received funding from ExxonMobil and Koch family foundations). A Greenpeace investigation into another conference speaker, astrophysicist Willie Soon, found that between 2002 and 2010, 100% of his new research

grants come from fossil fuel interests. . . . The people
paid to amplify the views of the scientists—in blogs,
op-eds, and television appearances—are bankrolled
by many of the same sources.[6]

Do scientists' or lobbyists' receipt of funds from fossil-fuel
companies guarantee that they are incapable of independent
thinking on issues of climate change? Not necessarily. Even
Naomi Klein, always skeptical of corporate intentions, policies, and actions, agrees that the cause-effect relationship is
unclear. "There is no way of knowing exactly how the money
shapes the views of those who receive it or whether it does at
all," she writes in *This Changes Everything*. However, "We do
know that having a significant economic stake in the fossil fuel
economy makes one more prone to deny the reality of climate
change, regardless of political affiliation." This seems as likely
to be true for scientists as for anyone else. Klein notes that

> While 97% of active climate scientists believe humans
> are a major cause of climate change, the numbers are
> radically different among 'economic geologists'—
> scientists who study natural formations so that they
> can be commercially exploited by the extractive
> industries. Only 47% of these scientists believe in
> human-caused climate change. The bottom line
> is that we are all inclined to denial in the truth is
> too costly—whether emotionally, intellectually, or
> financially.[7]

There is abundant reason to believe that climate-change
deniers hold their opinions for reasons other than cognitive
dissonance alone. Evidence regarding The Heartland
Institute's cozy relationship with fossil fuel corporations is
disturbing enough. Worse is the evidence that although fossil-
fuel companies' executives are fully aware that the burning
of oil, coal, and similar products contribute significantly to

climate change, they routinely choose to ignore the evidence. Worst of all, some of these companies have actively suppressed the evidence. In a *New York Times* op-ed piece, for instance, Naomi Oreskes reports that Exxon (now Exxon Mobil) fostered a decades-long effort to obscure the connection between fossil fuels and global climate change. As Oreskes writes:

> Exxon (which became Exxon Mobil in 1999) was a leader in these campaigns of confusion. In 1989, the company helped to create the Global Climate Coalition to question the scientific basis for concern about climate change and prevent the United States from signing on to the international Kyoto Protocol to control greenhouse gas emissions. The coalition disbanded in 2002, but the disinformation continued. Journalists and scientists have identified more than 30 different organizations funded by the company that have worked to undermine the scientific message and prevent policy action to control greenhouse gas emissions.
>
> These efforts turned the problem from a matter of fact into a matter of opinion. When the Exxon chief executive, Lee Raymond, insisted in the late 1990s that the science was still uncertain, the media covered it, business leaders accepted it and the American people were confused.[8]

Ironically, some of Exxon's own scientists were among the first to predict catastrophic effects from climate change. Oreskes notes that

> In the 1980s, Exxon scientists collaborated with academic and government researchers to build climate models and understand their implications. When one researcher expressed the opinion that the impacts would be "well short of catastrophic," the director of

the Theoretical and Mathematical Sciences Laboratory at Exxon Research responded in a memo, "I think that this statement may be too reassuring." He said it was "distinctly possible" that the projected warming trend after 2030 "will indeed be catastrophic (at least for a substantial fraction of the earth's population)," a conclusion that most climate scientists now hold, assuming we continue business as usual.[9]

How did Exxon executives respond to their own scientists' warnings? "As the scientific community began to speak out more strongly," Oreskes notes, "first about the risks of unmitigated climate change and then about the fact that it was underway, Exxon executives and organizations funded by them embarked on a campaign designed to prevent governments from taking meaningful action. These activities continue today." Oreskes writes:

> [L]ike the tobacco industry—Exxon chose the path of disinformation, denial and delay. More damagingly, the company set a model for the rest of the industry. More than 30 years ago, Exxon scientists acknowledged in internal company memos that climate change could be catastrophic. Today, scientists who say the exact same thing are ridiculed in the business community and on the editorial page of *The Wall Street Journal.* [10]

≈ ≈ ≈

"This year [2016] has seen record hot global ocean temperatures . . . Air surface temperatures have also been shocking climate scientists. Yearly and monthly temperature records have been breaking regularly, with many of the records being broken by the biggest margins ever seen. 'It's pretty ugly when you look at it,' [James] Butler [director of global monitoring at the U.S. National Oceanographic and Atmospheric Administration] told The Guardian."

—Michael Slezak, *The Guardian* [11]

WE MAY NOT KILL OUR PLANET ALL AT ONCE, but we're clearly subjecting it, and ourselves, to cumulative, potentially irreversible toxicity. Will climate change extinguish all human life on earth? That's unlikely. Will a dramatically warmer climate that falls short of global catastrophe still have negative consequences? That's now certain. Larger and more severe hurricanes, more frequent and more violent tornadoes, more severe and widespread wildfires, longer and worse droughts, widespread flooding of coastal cities, acute damage to farmlands and thus to the food supply—all of these risks are consistent with climate scientists' predictions. If these predictions come true, the consequences will include many thousands of deaths, widespread economic stress, depletion of water supplies, agricultural shortfalls, malnutrition and famine, and the likelihood of armed conflicts as regions and nations squabble over resources. Modern civilization will suffer great damage, perhaps even general collapse, if the stresses grow severe enough.

How soon? Scientists aren't sure about the timetable, but the process is already under way. Precisely because this process is incremental, inconsistent, and unpredictable, the currently gradual changes foster complacency similar to a frog's state of mind while sitting in a water-filled kettle. There's no single Moment of Truth of the sort we would reach if an asteroid were to crash into the earth.

        🙠 🙠 🙠

"We live on a very nice planet. It will be a pity if we destroy it."

—Oliver Sacks [12]

TO WHAT DEGREE CAN I, OR ANYONE intervene when our civilization seems intent on suicide? What actions can I, or anyone, take when the entire human species seems intent on leaping to its death? Shall I write letters to my congressman and senators? I do that. Shall I join groups focusing on addressing environmental degradation? I've joined 350.org, Interfaith Power & Light, Citizens' Climate Lobby, and several other organizations focused on climate disruption. Shall I donate money to activist campaigns? I do that too. Shall I march in climate-change demonstrations? I've considered that and will probably follow through in the near future. If I take these and other actions—if all of us, for that matter, take our equivalent actions—will we succeed in pulling our species back from the brink?

Lacking any better ideas, I start writing letters to corporate CEOs and badger them about climate disruption. A standard assumption among many environmentalists is that corporations are a significant part of the climate-change problem. Abundant and growing evidence about the fossil fuel companies' disinformation campaigns. However, I can't imagine how we'll address climate disruption without an alliance between environmentalists and the corporate sector. Capitalism itself may (as Naomi Klein and other activists claim) be the primary engine for damaging the global environment; even so, I see no means of avoiding disaster without somehow enlisting the corporate sector to help reverse the process and address the damage. Maybe I'm just a delusional Don Quixote tilting with my pen at windmills—or at coal-fired generating plants—but, lacking any better idea, this is what I start to do.

"Dear Mr. Gates," I write to the founder of Microsoft, one of the richest people in the world (2018 net worth: $90 billion) but also an extraordinary philanthropist. "This letter concerns the looming disaster that faces our planet as a result of climate disruption." I then present my thought experiment about the asteroid and how that crisis, unlike the equivalent crisis of global warming, would surely prompt a worldwide mobilization to counter the threat. I ask my question about why our society seems unwilling to make a comparable response to the current dilemma. Then I go on to write:

> All of us know the old adage, "Don't kill the customers—it's bad for business." I'm sure you would agree with this analogous notion: "Don't destroy the planet—it's bad for business." In addition, your work through the Bill and Melinda Gates Foundation, including your admirable initiative to reduce or eliminate the global scourge of malaria, shows your genuine concern for human beings throughout the world. For this reason, I'm approaching you now to urge you, even beseech you, to step forward and mobilize an effort to counteract the huge and rapidly worsening threat of global catastrophe that will result from climate disruption.

After summarizing climate scientists' research into the earth's climate and quoting some of their dire conclusions about how reliance on fossil fuels will lead to widespread, severe ecological problems, I make a request to Mr. Gates:

> Since the Trump administration's policies regarding climate disruption are essentially to deny the scientific data, roll back any prior efforts to ameliorate the crisis, and pander to the fossil fuel industries in every possible way, I urge you to mobilize a private-sector response to the looming crisis. I urge you to:
>
> • Organize a council of your fellow Titans of Industry
>
> • Create a practical action plan for addressing climate disruption

- Coax, cajole, and persuade other corporate executives to grasp the magnitude of the crisis we face as a species, and

- Take short-term, intermediate-term, and long-term steps to diminish carbon emissions before the already serious changes in the global climate create an irreversible, cascading sequence of environmental degradations.

I send my letter and wait.

The response? Silence.

I'm not naïve enough to imagine that Bill Gates, ensconced in his trophy home in Medina, Washington, would have personally opened the envelope himself, read my letter, sat bolt upright, and exclaimed to Melinda: "Listen to this! A writer in Vermont says climate change is a *problem*." At best, a mailroom clerk at Microsoft headquarters has read what I sent . . . and has then summarily tossed my letter into the recycling bin. Still, the silence isn't acceptable.

I send equivalent letters to Jeff Bezos, Mark Zuckerberg, and Elon Musk. I send letters to George Soros, Carl Icahn, Carlos Slim, Sheldon Adelson, Steve Ballmer, and Jim Walton. I send a copy to Michael Bloomberg. I even send one to Charles Koch, the surviving brother of the über-rich Koch family. Surely even these moguls must grasp somewhere deep inside their bubbles of privilege and comfort that they, their families, and their friends will ultimately suffer the consequences of climate disruption. They, too, will reap the whirlwind when the global environment deteriorates from the rapid warming of the atmosphere, from the acidification of the oceans, from the desertification of large areas on several continents, from the rising sea levels, from the increasing violence of tornadoes and hurricanes, from the spread of drought in California, Australia, Africa, the Middle East—

Or perhaps they don't. Perhaps they grasp these threats but can't take them seriously. Perhaps they regard their own short-term profits as having priority over the long-term health of our planet. Perhaps they suffer from a delusion that wealth will somehow spare them from the consequences of climate disruption.

I receive no responses. None at all. Does the silence matter? Would my letters ever prompt any CEOs to take action? I'm aware that even if what I sent were to reach the intended recipients, which is unlikely, my comments and suggestions will seem little more than the utterances of yet another crank out there among the hoi polloi. What I find more troubling is that except for Michael Bloomberg, there's no sign in the news that any of these executives grasps how dire the situation has already become, much less how severely it will worsen in the future; or if they grasp the situation, that they're willing to take action.

≈ ≈ ≈

Amid the mastodonic wassail
I heard the voice of one small fossil
Who said, "Cheer up, world," and winked.
"It's kind of fun to be extinct."

—Ogden Nash (lyrics for
Camille Saint-Saëns's
"The Carnival of the Animals")

THE LONG-TERM CRISES WE FACE as a result of global climate disruption are so dire that they sap the power of metaphors to portray the crisis. Is our civilization's current state the equivalent of someone standing on a ledge and contemplating a leap to ease the pain of unbearable depression? No, our culture's drift toward calamity isn't a result of depression so much as a blithe disregard for reality. What, then, would provide a better image? Perhaps our dilemma is analogous to Germanwings Flight 9525, the Airbus A320 that crashed into a mountainside in the French Alps on March 24, 2015, killing all 150 persons on board. If so, we are all Co-pilot Andreas Lubitz preparing to commit simultaneous suicide and mass murder; we are the passengers in the cabin growing belatedly aware of an imminent catastrophe; we are Captain Patrick Sondenheimer bashing at the cockpit door in a desperate effort to regain control of the plane; and we are the aircraft itself making its final plunge.[13]

Or perhaps we most closely resemble skydivers who, though knowledgeable about the physics of gravity and descent, have grown delusional about the consequences of freefall because the immediate experience is so exhilarating. The sense of weightlessness! The illusion of flying! The delights of scanning the vast horizon! How could a terrible future arise from such a splendid present? Indeed, nothing bad is under way—yet—for those skydivers. And no civilization-threatening global calamity has befallen our planet—yet. As my brother-in-law Geoff helpfully pointed out to me some years ago: "Contrary to popular belief, falling isn't dangerous. Even falling many miles won't hurt you. It's the sudden stop at the bottom that's the problem."

Maybe this analogy comes closer to what we now face as a species. Even someone who jumps out of a plane suffers no ill effects during his or her descent. Only the end of the fall causes any damage. Perhaps the equivalent is true for us, too, as a species. Like skydivers, we can revel in our descent because it doesn't seem like falling at all; because falling feels instead like flying; because we can imagine ourselves somehow exempt from the laws of physics; and because the panorama that extends as far as we can see now inspires a delusion that this planet is limitless, and so is our time on earth.

Déjà, Presque, Jamais Vu?

How can we know things we have no way of knowing? How can we recall events we never experienced?

To put the situation in personal terms: why would a boy growing up in white-bread 1950's Denver develop spontaneous, powerful sense of connection with a Renaissance instrument he had never heard or even seen? Why would the same boy respond viscerally to discussions and images of World War I, a conflict that ended thirty-two years before his birth, that had no direct consequences for his family, and that had no discernible impact on his Middle American life?

Both situations make no sense. Neither has a clear explantion. Precisely because both seem nonsensical and inexplicable—and because I was the boy in question—I've often wondered what might clarify the situation.

IN CATCH-22, JOSEPH HELLER WRITES of Albert Taylor Chapman, "the chaplain," regarding the intense confusion that this character feels when he seems to perceive or remember experiences he can't have undergone. The chaplain doubts his own perceptions but attempts to make sense of them.

> For a few precious seconds, the chaplain tingled with a weird, occult sensation of having experienced the identical situation before in some prior time or existence. . . . *Déjà vu.* The subtle, recurring confusion between illusion and reality that was characteristic of paramnesia fascinated the chaplain, and he knew

a number of things about it. He knew, for example, that it was called paramnesia, and he was interested as well in such corollary optical phenomena as *jamais vu,* never seen, and *presque vu,* almost seen.

Mulling over these experiences, the chaplain considers their psychological and phenomenological import.

There was no mistaking the awesome implications of the chaplain's revelation: it was either an insight of divine origin or a hallucination; he was either blessed or losing his mind. Both prospects filled him with equal fear and depression. [Yet his experience] was neither *déjà vu, presque vu* nor *jamais vu.* It was possible that there were other *vus* of which he had never heard and that one of these other *vus* would explain succinctly the baffling phenomenon of which he had been both a witness and a part; it was even possible that none of what he thought had taken place, really had taken place, that he was dealing with an aberration of memory rather than of perception, that he never really had thought he had seen what he now thought he once did think he had seen, that his impression now that he once had thought so was merely the illusion of an illusion. . . [1]

This description may show the chaplain's struggle with, among other things, the possibility of reincarnation. Or does it? Are there other explanations for the sense of perceiving or recalling an event one can't have experienced?

WHEN I WAS EIGHT YEARS OLD, a picture in a book caught my attention. Volume K-L of *The World Book Encyclopedia,* 1938 edition, showed a picture of a long-haired woman playing a strange musical instrument. Wearing a dark velvet gown and smiling almost imperceptibly, she sat in a chair, held the instrument, and appeared to be plucking some of its many strings. The neck and strings gave it a slight resemblance to a mandolin, but the large pear-shaped body, the wide neck, and the angled tuning box made it strange, exotic, and unfamiliar. The article called this instrument a lute. I had never seen a lute before, or even a photo of a lute, yet I knew at once that I wanted to play one. More than wanted: *needed*.

I took the book to my parents, showed them the picture, and explained the urgency of my obtaining and playing this mysterious instrument. "People don't actually play the lute anymore," my father said. "They're all in museums now." I pointed out that the photo showed a real woman playing a real instrument. My mother said, "She's posing with it. She's a model." I found this explanation unconvincing. Nor did I agree with my mother's further comments: "She's *pretending* to play it. Nobody really plays the lute nowadays." My father made his own effort to clarify: "Some instruments used to be played long ago but aren't any more. They've gone extinct, just like the dinosaurs." I rejected their baffling unwillingness to see the obvious. "*She's* playing it," I insisted, "and I want to play one, too."

Their reactions surprised me. Both of my parents were university professors and cultured people. Until this incident occurred, they had always responded with great warmth to my expressions of artistic curiosity. I had never experienced their nixing a request to let me explore the arts. Now my pleas went nowhere. They praised my interest in music but urged me to take up an instrument that wasn't "extinct," such as the violin.

The puzzle remains: why would an eight-year-old American kid growing up in the 1950's become obsessed with the lute? A kid in Denver, yet, a small city still emerging at the time from its cow-town past? My interests were typical of any other American boy's during that era: riding my bike, climbing trees, playing cops 'n' robbers, building model airplanes, and watching the Buck Rogers serials each Saturday at the local RKO theater. It's true that I spent hours exploring my parents' classical 78's and LPs, an activity that pleased them, and they encouraged my curiosity. But their collection didn't include albums of pre-baroque repertoire. Except for a few bits of Christmas music (the Coventry carol comes to mind) I had never heard any pieces dating from the Renaissance. Where did my fascination with the lute come from? Why was my attraction so immediate, my obsession so intense? Why did I feel such a strong connection that it never diminished? In 1965, when the mid-twentieth century early-music revival reached even Denver, my discovery of Julian Bream's LP *The Golden Age of Elizabethan Lute Music* inspired me to acquire a lute, study its technique, and make a lifelong avocation of its repertoire. I continue to play renaissance and baroque lutes even as I now approach age seventy.

MY ONLY BOYHOOD EXPERIENCE relevant to World War I involved watching a handful of American former doughboys march down Denver's Fifteenth Street in a Veterans' Day parade during the mid- or late 1950's. I recall how peculiar they looked in their metal salad-bowl helmets and ace-bandaged calves. These men must have been in their 60's and 70's. The far more numerous, more impressive soldiers in the parade hailed from my parents' generation—the World War Two veterans who, thirty- and forty-something at the time, marched in their uniforms and rode in jeeps that I recognized from movies of that era. Almost all the kids I knew came from families in which the fathers had served in the recent war. Discussions of World War II were frequent and often intense. Yet it was World War I that somehow concerned, disturbed, and alarmed me.

A COMMON EXPLANATION for similar experiences throughout history has been the concept of reincarnation. According to this theory, people may remember places, events, and other human beings as a result of encounters not just in this lifetime but in one or more lived earlier. Many cultures have posited the notion that each person has had prior, perhaps countless, lifetimes. In some respects, reincarnation may provide an explanation for common experiences that are otherwise baffling, even bizarre. A Denver schoolboy in the mid-1950's longs to play a musical instrument he had never seen or heard. Why? Perhaps he actually knew about lutes during an earlier lifetime. This same boy, as well as the man he became, grows obsessed with and upset about a long-past war. Why? Perhaps he had experienced that conflict in some way or other. Or so, at least, proponents of reincarnation would claim. It's as plausible, however—far more plausible—that these and other fascinations result from the human capacities of imagination, curiosity, and compassion. These attributes are powerful in their own right. One needn't have experienced something first hand to find it compelling, intriguing, wrenching, or delightful; one can vividly grasp by other means what other people have experienced at other times.

RESEARCH UNDERTAKEN by the Pew Forum on Religion and Public Life reveals that almost 25%Americans believe in reincarnation.[2] This level of belief is a significant departure from the traditional Judaeo-Christian assumptions predominant in the U.S. throughout most of this nation's history. When people indicate that they "believe in reincarnation," however, a follow-up question should be: *which concept* of reincarnation?" Beliefs regarding reincarnation have taken many forms throughout history. The Hindu concept derives from Upanishadic writings (7th through 5th centuries BCE) that posit an *atman* (impersonal self) reincarnated into other bodies in accordance with one's *karma* (accumulations of positive or negative actions). By contrast, Buddhism denies the existence of a permanent self but accepts reincarnation as the transfer of *karma* from one life to the next, much as a flame can be transferred from one candle to another. Non-Hindu, non-Buddhist cultures—such as the Yoruba in West Africa, the Zoroastrians in ancient Persia, and the Teutons, Celts, and Gauls in pre-Christian Europe—have included other concepts of reincarnation within their belief systems. So have some classical and medieval traditions within Western cultures: Platonism, Neo-platonism, Hermitism, and Catharism, among others. Nineteenth and twentieth-century writers (such as Madame Blavatsky and Gurdjieff) rummaged among these many concepts to stitch together their own theoretical quilts.[3]

Twentieth- and early twenty-first-century notions often seem a kind of Reincarnation Lite. "Far from being a torment out of which man has to escape by any price through abolishing personhood," writes Ernest Valea, "New Age thinking sees reincarnation as an eternal progression of the soul toward higher levels of spiritual knowledge."

> The concept of reincarnation seems to offer one of the most attractive explanations of humanity's origin and destiny. . . . [R]eincarnation is a source of great comfort, especially for those who seek liberation on the exclusive basis of their inner resources. It gives assurance for continuing one's existence in further lives and thus having a renewed chance to attain liberation.[4]

DO THE VARIETIES AND THE "SOFTNESS" of contemporary beliefs about reincarnation mean that they have no validity? The answer to that question isn't clear. I've always been leery of New Age notions, but I'm also reluctant to dismiss the entire issue out of hand. Years ago, a friend from New York, age ninety at the time, said, "After I die I'll be dead for a long time, so I don't need to practice." (My friend's use of the word "practice" with regard to being dead referred to the possibility of his moving to Florida.) But what if the opposite is true? What if following death we're *alive* for a long time? What if notions of death as total cessation are as presumptuous as notions that the soul (or some aspect of consciousness) lives on? Despite being far-fetched, the possibilities of an afterlife are sufficiently important to warrant consideration.

ON ONE LEVEL, AT LEAST, reincarnation is a given. Our planet contains a finite number of atoms. Except for what meteors keep adding to the mix, all of the matter on Earth has been here for billions of years. The rocks, dirt, water, bacteria, fungi, viruses, plants, animals, and people are all made from the same stockpile of atoms. Whatever else, nature is a vast recycling center. You and I and everyone else came into existence made of the same chemical components that had previously constituted rocks, dirt, water, bacteria, fungi, viruses, plants, animals, and people. When we die, our bodies will break down into component atoms that nature will reconstitute into new bacteria, fungi, viruses, plants, animals, and people. Even if there is no other Great Wheel of Birth, Death, and Rebirth, the great wheel of nature is constantly turning.

WHAT ABOUT OTHER KINDS of reincarnation? What about the concept that a human being's immaterial soul can be reborn into the physical substance of another person? It's a vexedly difficult concept to prove or disprove. "The problem with reincarnation," writes Alex Lickerman, M.D., "is twofold: 1) we have, as of yet, no way to verify it prospectively in an objective manner, and 2) we have no mechanism to explain how reincarnation might occur."[5]

However, a scattering of trained researchers delved into these issues from the mid-twentieth century on. One psychiatrist who employed rigorous methods to study reincarnation "in an objective manner" was Ian Stevenson. A Canadian based at the University of Virginia School of Medicine for fifty years, Stevenson chaired the department of psychiatry from 1957 to

1967, held the Carlson Chair in Psychiatry from 1967 to 2001, and continued working as a Research Professor of Psychiatry from 2002 until his death in 2007.

Stevenson founded and directed UVA's Division of Perceptual Studies, a program that focused on investigating paranormal phenomena. In this capacity, Stevenson concentrated primarily on research into reincarnation—specifically, on investigating cases of children throughout the world who claimed to remember past lives. His book *Twenty Cases Suggestive of Reincarnation,* for instance, argues that some case histories of people experiencing phobias, philias, unusual abilities, and illnesses can't be fully explained in terms of heredity or the environment. Stevenson believed that reincarnation provided a third possible explanation. A bequest he received in 1968 funded Stevenson's subsequent research, including extensive travels (sometimes up to 55,000 miles a year), which led to his collecting three thousand case studies of children in places ranging from Africa to Alaska. A *Washington Post* article following Stevenson's death in 2007 summarized the nature of his research:

> In interviewing witnesses and reviewing documents, Dr. Stevenson searched for alternate ways to account for the testimony: that the child came upon the information in some normal way, that the witnesses were engaged in fraud or self-delusion, that the correlations were the result of coincidence or misunderstanding. But in scores of cases, Dr. Stevenson concluded that no normal explanation sufficed.[6]

Responses to Stevenson's research were mixed. *Twenty Cases Suggestive of Reincarnation,* as well as his other books and articles, received considerable criticism and at best guarded support from the medical and psychiatric communities. A few respectful articles appeared in *The Journal of the American Medical Association* and *The Journal of Nervous and Mental Disease* during the mid- and late 1970's. Most scientists, however, derided or ignored Stevenson's work. According to an obituary in *The New York Times*, his detractors perceived him as "earnest, dogged, but ultimately misguided, led astray by gullibility, wishful thinking and a tendency to see science where others saw superstition." Critics suggested variously that either the children or the parents whom Stevenson interviewed had deceived him, that he was too willing to believe his respondents, or that he had asked them leading questions. Other critics noted that Stevenson's findings were subject to "confirmation bias"—the tendency to select or reject data in accordance with pre-determined criteria—and that Stevenson didn't present cases that failed to support his hypothesis or counted against it. Leonard Angel, a philosopher of religion, told *The New York Times* that Stevenson failed to meet conventional standards for social-science research.[7]

Among the scientists who expressed skepticism about this line of research but who nevertheless didn't dismiss it altogether was astronomer Carl Sagan. Even though Sagan was a founding member of a group founded to debunk unscientific claims, he wrote in his book *The Demon-Haunted World* that "There are three claims in the [parapsychology] field which, in my opinion, deserve serious study," of which one was the phenomenon "that young children sometimes report details of a previous life, which upon checking turn out to be accurate and which they could not have known about in any other way than reincarnation."[8]

IN LIGHT OF THESE ISSUES, what should we make of the Tibetan Buddhist tradition of *tulkus*? As Ken McLeod states in a recent article, "'*Tulku*' is the Tibetan word for *nirmanakaya*, the form aspect [i.e., the physical manifestation] of a Buddha [an enlightened being]. In modern times the term has come to refer to a person who is recognized as the reincarnation of a former spiritual teacher. . . " McLeod goes on to describe the *tulku* system as a means "of identifying and developing spiritual talent to provide for the continuity of the tradition." Specifically, this system involves a process through which monks locate a child assumed to be a reincarnation of a recently deceased lama.

> When a high lama shows signs of [impending death], his disciples request him to reincarnate and continue his noble work of teaching the Doctrine and liberating ignorant beings. If the lama sees benefit in his being reborn in the same area, he accepts the request and reincarnates accordingly. Subsequently, a child is sought and the candidate who passes the series of traditional tests is formally recognized as the tulku, or reincarnation of the deceased lama.
>
> In most cases, the process of recognizing a *tulku* is begun by consulting a high lama and/or oracle for indications as to where to look. If they see that the *tulku* has already reincarnated, they may indicate the place, age of the child, and sometimes his home or family. . . . Only those candidates who survive this preliminary assessment continue to the more detailed and intensive tests. As the ultimate aim is to recognize the correct reincarnation, great care is taken throughout to ensure that the real reincarnate is among the remaining candidates. [9]

The investigation process involves monks setting forth from their monastery to visit families in which children may be the possible reincarnation of the late lama. This process includes showing the children a selection of objects among which are some of the deceased lama's own possessions. Prospective *tulkus* must choose the right objects to prove that they recognize what they owned in a prior lifetime.

The test usually conducted on the final candidates

includes checking whether the child remembers anything related to the previous lama, whether the child can recognize some possessions the previous lama has regularly used, whether he can recognize close disciples and attendants of the previous lama, as well as carefully studying the child's personality. In addition to these external tests, more penetrating inner and secret tests employing meditative insight are conducted by capable and experienced masters. In fact, the external tests are regarded as confirming and secondary to the inner and secret tests. The final decision, based on all these findings, is made by an authoritative lama.

According to Tibetan Buddhist assumptions, most children assumed to be reincarnated lamas remember and speak about their past lives, correctly recognize persons and objects closely related to their previous incarnations, and clearly reflect, through natural behavior, their deep familiarity with the Buddhist teachings. "For instance," McLeod writes, "the present Dalai Lama when four years old directly recognized two members of the search party, and correctly distinguished objects that had belonged to the Thirteenth Dalai Lama." [10]

This selection test is only one aspect of evaluating candidates to identify the *tulku*. Actual identification as a *tulku* hinges on other issues as well, some of which are rigorous.

To secular Westerners, however, as well as to some Buddhists, the entire *tulku* process seems bizarre, unsettling, and perhaps abusive, since a child's "successful" passing of the tests results in his removal from his family home and relocation to a monastery. Some of these boys are as young as four or five years old. (The current Dalai Lama, for instance, was only two when he left his family of origin; he began his monastic education at age six.) Traditional Tibetan culture considers a child's selection as a *tulku* to be a great honor. But do all parents approve of their child's removal from the family? How do the boys themselves feel about having to leave? Apparently the responses are more mixed than generally assumed.[11] In these and other respects, the notion of assessing past-life connections is both intriguing and disturbing. It resembles Ian Stevenson's research in some respects—that is, in focusing on children's possible past-life experiences—but with drastic consequences for the boys in question.

ONE ALTERNATIVE TO SOCIAL SCIENCE-BASED RESEARCH into re-incarnation is "past-life regression therapy." According to its proponents, this is a practical method for first-hand exploration of what they regard as earlier lifetimes. As one summary of the process describes it:

> Past life regression is a technique that uses hypnosis to recover what practitioners believe are memories of past lives or incarnations . . . Past-life regression is typically undertaken either in pursuit of a spiritual experience, or in a psychotherapeutic setting. Most advocates loosely adhere to beliefs about reincarnation, though religious traditions that incorporate reincarnation generally do not include the idea of repressed memories of past lives.
>
> The technique used during past-life regression involves the subject answering a series of questions while hypnotized to reveal identity and events of alleged past lives . . . .[12]

Ann C. Barham, a popular practitioner of past-life regression therapy, states her beliefs more bluntly and enthusiastically:

> Modern past life therapy is based on the premise that we are all eternal beings who experience physical life on earth in a series of human bodies and their associated personalities. As eternal souls, we

carry forward the experiences and lessons learned from one human lifetime to another. . . . [We] are involved in choosing aspects of each life as a means of expanding our experiences, learning the lessons we have set out for ourselves, and continuing our ongoing involvement with various other souls with whom we are strongly connected. . . . In addition to resolving these experiences from the past that are blocking our progress and happiness now, past life work is also very useful in bringing forth strengths and positive experiences from prior lifetimes that can actually enhance our current abilities and confidence. Our personalities can help us reach our full potential now![13]

Betty Moore-Hafter, another proponent of past-life regression therapy, succinctly summarizes the practice: "Past life regression focuses on discovering the origins of a problem and 'going back' to bring healing to the original situation. Past life regression allows access to past lives, real or symbolic, which in some cases hold the keys to resolving current issues." [14]

In short, past-life regression has become a treatment modality among New Age-oriented psychotherapists. Ann Barham, among other advocates of this approach, claim that it has now entered the mainstream. However, as one skeptic notes, "Past life regression is widely rejected as a psychiatric treatment by clinical psychiatrists and psychologists. A 2006 survey found that a majority of a sample of doctoral level mental health professionals rated 'Past Lives' therapy as 'certainly discredited' as a treatment for mental or behavioral disorders. Another states, "While it is true that many patients *recall* past lives, it is highly probable that their memories are *false memories*. The memories are from experiences in this life, pure products of the imagination, intentional or unintentional suggestions from the hypnotist, or confabulations." [15]

What is the past-life regression process like? Betty Moore-Hafter describes her own methodology:

> In a typical past life regression session, you are gently guided through hypnotherapy to find an inner experience from an earlier time. The stories that emerge carry powerful emotion and heartfelt meaning. Past life regression allows access to deep levels of the personality where emotional patterns are rooted and core beliefs held. Healing work at this level includes clearing the negative emotion and distorted beliefs . . . Sometimes the physical body has been holding the stress, and as it is cleared, people are permanently freed of pain or tension. We usually end with further hypnotherapy to bring healing, wholeness and harmony to all parts of you and restore the connection with your True Self. [16]

FEW PRACTITIONERS within the psychiatric, psychological, and scientific communities of view this methodology in a favorable light. The American Psychological Association's *APA Dictionary of Psychology,* for instance, includes this entry:

> Past-Life Regression. A highly controversial hypnotic regression technique in which a person is encouraged to move back in time to reexperience a supposed previous existence. Therapists who conduct past-life regression believe that the psychological and physical problems (e.g., phobias, insomnia) . . . can be understood and resolved by discovering their origins in the experiences (e.g., traumas, unresolved conflicts, mistakes) of previous lives. Most hypnotherapists are skeptical of the practice and do not recognize it as a legitimate therapeutic tool. They claim that individuals' memories of past lives are the product of fantasy, imaginative role

playing, the expectations and suggestions implicitly conveyed to them by the hypnotist, or unconsciously produced confabulations constructed from personal knowledge, familiar places, events, television shows, novels, and other sources. [17]

Similarly, an organization called Science-Based Medicine categorically dismisses everything about past-life regression therapy, including the notion of reincarnation itself:

> In past life regression therapy, therapists use hypnosis, leading questions, and strong suggestions to encourage patients to imagine that reincarnation is real and to imagine their past lives. Events and people from past lives are blamed for symptoms and problems in the patient's current life. Finding a past life cause for current problems supposedly helps patients deal with them. The technique is also used in healthy people to promote spiritual advancement and self-understanding. There is no such thing as reincarnation, and the memories of past lives are nothing but fantasy. [18]

Even Ian Stevenson issued an explicit disapproval of past-life regression therapy. Shortly before his death, he wrote:

> Many persons who attach no importance whatever to their dreams—realizing that most of them are merely images of the dreamer's subconscious mind without correspondence to any other reality—nevertheless believe that whatever emerges during hypnosis can invariably be taken at face value. In fact, the state of a person during hypnosis resembles [dreaming] in many ways. . . . The subconscious parts of the mind are released from ordinary inhibitions and they may then present in dramatic form a new "personality."

If the subject has been instructed by the hypnotist—explicitly or implicitly—to "go back to another place and time" or given some similar guidance, the new "personality" may appear to be one of another period of history. Such evoked "previous personalities" may be extremely plausible both to the person having the experience and to other persons watching him or her. Experiments by [psychologist Robert] Baker and by Nicholas Spanos and his colleagues have shown how easily different suggestions given by a hypnotist can influence the features of the "previous personality" in conformity with suggestions.

Stevenson goes on to state:

In fact, . . . nearly all such hypnotically evoked "previous personalities" are entirely imaginary just as are the contents of most dreams. They may include some accurate historical details, but these are usually derived from information the subject has acquired normally through reading, radio and television programs, or other sources. The subject may not remember where he obtained the information included, but sometimes this can be brought out in other sessions with hypnosis designed to search for the sources of the information used in making up the "previous personality." Experiments by E. Zolik and by R. Kampman and R. Hirvenoja have demonstrated this phenomenon. [19]

In addition, Stevenson notes that "A marked emotional experience during the hypnotic regression provides no assurance that memories of a real previous life were recovered. The subjective experience of reliving a previous life may be impressive to the person having the experience, and yet the 'previous life' may be a fantasy, like most of our dreams."

∼ ∼ ∼

IN JULY OF 2008, I accompanied my wife on a business trip to Brussels. We explored the city for two days; then Edith settled in to work with her client for several days more. Footloose and alone, I explored the capital during my free time that week. Another option occurred to me: touring World War I battle-fields. I'm not generally interested in military history, but my longstanding obsession with the Great War made this conflict an exception. For this reason, I booked a one-day tour of the strategically critical Ypres Salient located about eighty miles west of Brussels. There I met up with Annette, a guide from Camalou Battlefield Tours, who drove me to various sites and explained events that transpired during battles that engulfed the area from October of 1914 almost until the Armistice in No-vember of 1918.

Given my dark fascination with the First World War, I was aware that this excursion might be evocative and upsetting. But evocative of what? Upsetting about what? Years of reading about the war had given me a substantial overview of that four-year catastrophe; I had often responded emotionally as well as intellectually to what I'd learned; and, for lack of any better word, I had resonated to this wretched episode in modern history. What did that resonance mean? Did it mean anything beyond my feeling a general disgust toward human beings' propensity for mutual slaughter? Pondering these questions over a period of decades, I hadn't reached any conclusions that could explain how or why I might feel such a specific, visceral resonance to a war that ended thirty-two years before my birth. Yet I felt that resonance. Even when approaching Ypres in a Belgian intercity train, I grew tense, confused, and emotional. Rolling past one of the area's dozens of immaculate military cemeteries suddenly brought me to tears. No comparable response had ever hit me with such intensity in any other historical setting. I have visited dozens of other graveyards in a dozen countries spanning a thousand years of history. Why would my psyche now feel torn asunder by the sight of all those neatly arrayed white markers?

For most of July second, Annette took me to battlefields, ruins, bunkers, and cemeteries. We toured Hill 60, the site of a protracted battle during April and May of 1915. We visited the town of Wijtshaate, once east of No-Man's Land, where restored wickerwork trenches provide a glimpse of German fortifications. We visited British bunkers and viewed the remnants of Allied trenches. A particularly bizarre side trip led us up to the Messine Ridge, once a major German redoubt on high ground and the target of a remarkable British offensive. For weeks during the late spring of 1917, crews of English, Canadian, Australian, and New Zealand miners tunneled under the ridge, deposited twenty-six mines and 454 metric tons of ammonal explosives, and detonated the charges early on the morning of June 7th. 11,000 Germans died in the first wave of explosions. The ensuing battle resulted in an estimated total of almost 23,000 German casualties.[20] Allied casualties included 28,000 British and over 11,000 Commonwealth troops. Yet now, almost ninety years later, what lay before me was an idyllic rural landscape—a farmhouse, a barn, a meadow, and extensive cornfields. The beauty of the place was deceptive: unexploded ordnance lies buried in the soil. Even as I walked among knee-high plants in the field, I spotted balls of lead shrapnel in the dirt as easily as if noticing kernels of last year's corn. The contrast between the hideous past and the bucolic present felt jarring and bizarre. The once bomb-churned mud that had drowned unwary soldiers now nurtured lush crops. The once-splintered stands of trees had rejuvenated into peaceful woods. The once-gaping craters scattered across the fields now served as ponds to provide water for livestock. Later, Annette and I visited several memorials, including the massive Tyne Cot Cemetery, where 11,965 Allied troops lie buried. The Commonwealth War Graves Commission designed and created Tyne Cot during the late Nineteen Teens and Twenties in memory of Allied personnel, and to this day the same organization meticulously maintains the vast rows of gravestones—what the poet Edgar Bowers has called "the perfect order trusted to the dead." [21]

My reaction to these places? I felt shaken, unnerved, and exhausted, but at no point did I find my mind providing, or even hinting at, anything I could call specific recollections. At no point did I feel a *personal* connection to the Flemish battlefields. At no point did I feel a past life welling up into my consciousness. Yet I felt upset. Was there any reason *not* to be upset? Four years of fighting in the Ypres Salient alone—a region no bigger than metropolitan Los Angeles—had caused the deaths of at least 400,000 human beings and had resulted in over a million total casualties. Overall, World War I killed at least seven million civilians and ten million military personnel, as well causing as approximately twenty million other casualties. Why shouldn't this colossal squandering of human lives move me—move anyone—to tears? I needn't have experienced this calamity during a prior lifetime to feel the loss. That being said, I still felt aware of a puzzling magnetism that had drawn me to Flanders in the first place, and to the physical and emotional heaviness that weighed on me as I left.

My notes for that long day of battlefield tourism end inconclusively: "Inner question regarding what this is about: an attempt to recall events I have never experienced—or simply the effects of a vivid imagination?"

READING THIS ACCOUNT of my trip to Flanders, a proponent of reincarnation might respond: "Of *course* you didn't remember what happened to you in the Ypres Salient! You probably weren't there in a past life. You didn't visit the right place to evoke any memories. What happened to you back then probably didn't happen in Flanders. Maybe it happened in Germany—or in the Middle East, or in Russia. Maybe you weren't even a soldier during the Great War. Maybe you were a soldier's wife who lost your husband. Or a child who lost your father." And so forth. Proponents of reincarnation would, in short, have confident explanations for my inability to derive a specific, personal sense of connection. Perhaps their confidence is presumptuous. On the other hand, I can't rule out that they have a point. I've always found skepticism a sound approach when exploring the world, but skepticism alone doesn't prove that something doesn't exist.

AFTER WEEKS OF READING proponents' and critics' remarks about past-life regression, I decided that assessing this approach to reincarnation shouldn't happen only at a distance. I continued to feel skeptical about this methodology. I remained unsure that it offers even a window, much less a doorway, into past lives. I remained agnostic. Yet I now felt that any further investigation must not just review of other people's conjecture and experiments but should also include some kind of first-hand experience. For this reason I did some research, I located several practitioners, and I learned as much as possible about their backgrounds, interests, and approaches. I contacted one of them—Betty Moore-Hafter, quoted earlier—because she seemed interesting and flexible in her attitudes toward the past-lives regression modality. Located in Burlington, Vermont, an hour's drive from where I live, Betty's practice would also be convenient for in-person discussions. An initial phone call put me at ease: Betty's description of past-lives regression therapy was succinct, articulate, unpretentious, and free of New Age jargon. When I informed her that I am agnostic about reincarnation—"both open-minded and skeptical," as I put it—she responded, "You're right where I think it's best to be: without preconceptions." She outlined the possible outcomes of a past-lives therapy session and explained the sequences of steps it entails. After further questions asked and answered, I booked a single three-hour session. Three weeks later, on a frosty October day, I drove to Burlington for my session with Betty.

Late-sixties in an age, slim, white-haired, and casually elegant in attire, Betty was clearly warm, curious, and enthusiastic about her therapeutic practice. I liked her from the start and felt comfortable with her approach to past-life regression. I repeated my comment from the earlier phone call that I am both open-minded and skeptical about reincarnation, hence agnostic that the past-life regression modality offers access to memories from a prior lifetime. I stressed, however, that I was willing to give it a try. We then discussed my background—part of a screening process, I assumed, to rule out trauma and other potentially confounding issues. My answers didn't seem to prompt any concerns in Betty's mind. So, after I signed a standard consent form, we proceeded to the regression process itself.

This approach involves fairly standard methods of hypnotic induction. Once I settled into a recliner chair, Betty guided me through a series of induction exercises. These felt familiar from deep-relaxation methods I've used myself during studies of yoga and meditation. The first involved imagining pure light moving from the top of my head through my skull, across the areas of my face, down my neck, into my shoulders and arms, into my torso, down my back, into my belly, and so forth. The process was calming both physically and psychologically. Everything Betty said was comfortable, reassuring, and pleasant. I quickly entered a state of simultaneous deep relaxation and acute alertness—what some Buddhists call *samastha,* or "calm abiding." With this phase now complete, Betty then made a series of guiding comments, which, according to the assumptions about past-life regression, lead the subject deeper into the unconscious. The process involves imagining that one sees a doorway, opens a door, sees a staircase, descends the stairs, and reaches a subterranean place. A hallway stretches out ahead. On each side of the hallway are closed doors. One proceeds down the hallway, selects a door, and opens it. By this means one gains access to a past life and memories about it.

The catch for me, however, was that I didn't have any of the anticipated experiences at any step of this sequence. I didn't see the first doorway, the staircase, the second doorway, the hallway, or the closed doors. Betty asked, "What are you seeing?" I answered, "Foggy darkness." By this phrase I meant what I see routinely in a dark room: no object, no substance, just shadowy non-light. At a later stage of the process, I described the same phenomenon as "grainy darkness." In short, I saw more or less nothing. Betty offered some further prompts about the hall and the doorways. She asked other questions. Try as I might, however, I didn't find these prompts leading to any visual experience. Neither did I hear anything. Nor did I feel any emotional response to what was happening. I simply felt relaxed, comfortable, curious, and attentive. At some point, Betty asked, "What are you experiencing?" My response: "Nothing." We started to discuss the situation more amply than earlier. I could tell that she felt disconcerted by what was happening—or, more accurately, by what wasn't. When she asked, "Are you comfortable with proceeding?" I answered, "Yes, but I really need a bathroom break first." (As someone commented snarkily during the 1960s: "It's hard to have a higher spiritual experience when you're having a lower corporeal experience.")

I left her office briefly, used the bathroom, and returned. I sensed yet again that Betty was feeling perplexed or confused about the process so far. To put her at ease, I commented, "Sorry if I'm a tough nut to crack."

"Don't apologize," she responded. "I've just never experienced anything quite like this."

"I hope you'll believe me when I say I'm not willfully resisting."

"I believe you." Then she added, "I'm going to have to think this through."

After some further discussion, however, during which we speculated about our options, I told her that I wanted to follow her own hunches—specifically, by going ahead with whatever method she thought might be effective. She suggested some other modes of hypnotic induction. I agreed to this approach. So, once I had settled into the recliner once again, she proceeded.

One of these methods included a more dialogic process of induction. As before, this felt comfortable; I didn't resist. When we worked through a sequence of steps that involved descending once again into deeper layers of the unconscious, what I experienced once again was essentially—nothing. I saw grainy darkness but nothing else. At some point, however, I perceived a slight change. This involved seeing a grid-like structure resembling the dividers between window panes in a large 18th or 19th-century window. This subtle image was pale and unclear, just a rectilinear structure in or beyond the grainy darkness. It lingered. Betty asked some questions. What might this grid be made of? Was I was looking into a house or building or out of one? I said, "Out of." However, I saw no other features that suggested anything else about the place or its surroundings. Then this image, too, faded. Nothing else happened.

By now I could sense Betty hesitating, perhaps even grasping at hypnotic straws. She started asking questions about which historical era interested me. What eras of the past felt powerful? I commented, "That's a big question, isn't it? So much history." She asked about aspects of different eras. I began to feel for the first time that these were leading questions. Even so, I decided to gamble: "Well, I've always wondered why someone born in 1950 would feel obsessed with World War I." This comment, for better or worse, gave Betty a handle to grasp. She asked more questions. "Do you have any sense of that war from the standpoint of a soldier?"

"Unclear."

"Do you have a sense of it from the standpoint of a soldier's wife?"

"Unclear."

"From the standpoint of a soldier's child?"

"Unclear."

"What place affected by the war draws your attention?"

"Flanders."

This comment led a long discussion of Flanders—the destruction there, the years of suffering. We were off and running, with lots of comments back and forth about this aspect of the war. But the very nature of this discussion concerned me: a shift into a phase when Betty's questions shaped what was happening rather than just let it happen. Regardless, I decided to go with the flow. I responded to her questions. Even so, I felt little or no emotional engagement with the process. I was only going through the motions. I felt no connection with World War I as an experience—less so, certainly, than I had felt during my actual visit to Flanders. The discussion continued, but on some level I had already disengaged. I hadn't regressed into a past life; I was focusing once again on my present life.

WHAT, IF ANYTHING did my past-life session prove? That reincarnation doesn't exist? No. That memories of a past life are impossible? No. That past-life regression therapy generates delusions, not memories? No. It's altogether possible that reincarnation doesn't exist, that one can't have memories of a past life, that past-life regression therapy generates delusions, not memories. But my brief, one-time experience doesn't prove any of these conclusions. *Absence of evidence isn't evidence of absence,* as the adage goes among scientists, lawyers, and philosophers alike. In the context of my one instance of past-life regression therapy, all I proved is that no aspect of *my* experience suggested recollections of a past life. Everything else about the occasion was—to be blunt—inconclusive.

I'm not surprised by this outcome. My experience was brief, the outcome ambiguous, the resulting impressions limited. Nothing that came of it allows my drawing clear conclusions. However, the very notion of inconclusiveness raises a tricky personal issue. Many years ago, my girlfriend at the time criticized me for one of the many aspects of my personality she found exasperating: "You're always so *pleased* when life is inconclusive."

"I'm not *pleased*," I told her, "just not surprised. Life often *is* inconclusive."

"But you *like* it when things aren't clear-cut."

"I wouldn't say I like it. I just see inconclusiveness as more common than clarity."

Decades later, I still hold that assumption. Many experiences suggest interesting, even fascinating possibilities, but I don't regard those possibilities as definitive. Life *is* inconclusive.

Or does this attitude simply reflect my own confirmation bias? When experiences are ambiguous, I can say once again: See? Life is so inconclusive!

Which brings me back to the questions arising from my session with Betty Moore-Hafter. What does it mean if I have experiences during a past-life regression that suggest memories of a prior lifetime? What does it mean if I have no memories during a session? Or only vague feelings? Or no responses at all?

Unlike those who have clear opinions on this matter, I still can't feel sure. Some people clearly do have past-life regression experiences that suggest recollections of events preceding birth. However, such experiences offer no definitive proof of prior lifetimes. Psychological processes can explain to some degree what people perceive and feel during past-life regression. According to one article,

> The use of hypnosis and suggestive questions can tend to leave the subject particularly likely to hold distorted or false memories. Once created, the memories are indistinguishable from memories based on events that occurred during the subject's life. Memories reported during past-life regression have been investigated and [have] revealed historical inaccuracies that are easily explained through a basic knowledge of history, elements of popular culture, or

books that discuss historical events. . . . Psychologists
state that the "memories" recovered by techniques
like past-life regression are the result of cryptomnesia:
narratives created by the subconscious mind using
imagination, forgotten information and suggestions
i   from the therapist. [22]

Memories created under hypnosis are indistinguishable
from actual memories and can be more vivid.

While it is true that many [past-life regression]
patients *recall* past lives, it is highly probable that
their memories are *false* memories. The memories
are from experiences in this life, pure products of the
imagination, intentional or unintentional suggestions
from the hypnotist, or confabulations.

Attitudes about reincarnation also exert an outsized influence on outcomes during past-life regression therapy.

Psychologist Robert Baker demonstrated that *belief
in reincarnation* is the greatest predictor of whether a
subject would have a past-life memory while under
past life regression hypnotherapy. Furthermore,
Baker demonstrated that the subject's expectations
significantly affect the past-life regressive session.
He divided a group of 60 students into three groups.
He told the first group that they were about to
experience an exciting new therapy that could help
them uncover their past lives. Eighty-five per cent
in this group were successful in "remembering" a
past life. He told the second group that they were to
learn about a therapy which may or may not work
to engender past-life memories. In this group, the
success rate was 60%. He told the third group that the

therapy was crazy and that normal people generally do not experience a past life. Only 10% of this group had a past-life "memory." [23]

❧   ❧   ❧

I HAD A DREAM RECENTLY in which an unfamiliar man followed me into a dark hallway. I grew fearful and tried to escape but couldn't move. Then the man rushed me, grabbed me from behind, and tried to strangle me. I woke up suddenly, alarmed and gasping.

Hearing my description, a psychoanalyst might interpret the dream as follows: "This dream reflects Oedipal anxiety and anger. The man who tried to kill you represents your father. Your resistance against him represent your filial struggle to define yourself as a man." A Jungian analyst might comment: "The man represents the Shadow archetype, and his attack represents your effort to accommodate the dark side of your own psyche that is welling up from the unconscious." A neuropsychologist might tell me, "During REM sleep, the body enters a state of near-total paralysis, which is why dreams can include a sense of frightening immobility. The mind is aware of the body's inability to move, so it tells stories that explain this alarming state of being—stories about monsters, assailants, and other menacing presences. In your case, that normal state of involuntary immobility led to the story about a strange man attacking and strangling you. It's all part of the mind's effort to interpret physiological signals." And a past-life regression practitioner? He or she might well say, "The dream reflects evidence that you struggled with an assailant in a past life. This person may even have killed you during that lifetime, which is why the dream is so powerful and terrifying."

Of these modes of dream interpretation, I find only the neuro-psychological schema fully plausible. Some people will object to this set of assumptions: "It's too reductive." But the

Freudian and Jungian schemata, among others, are also reductive. The past-life interpretation is attractive but simplistic as well, for it ignores the complexity and power of the human imagination. By contrast, the neuropsychological schema is backed by abundant research and involves far less speculation than the others do.

The truth is, we still don't really know how the mind works. We don't even know what the mind *is*. After two or three thousand years of earnest speculation, our species is only now gaining a clearer sense of what consciousness is, what purposes it serves, and what it can explain about itself. Among other things, it's not clear whether consciousness is simply the side effect of electrical activity among countless neurons—or whether some aspect of conscious can survive the death of the physical body.

TO INVOKE THE CHAPLAIN IN CATCH-22, some experiences may be *déjà vu,* and if "already seen" thus imply a prior event or experience. Or perhaps they are *presque vu,* implying an event that one can almost but not quite perceive. Or perhaps, as Heller has the chaplain consider, it's possible that there are "other *vus* of which he had never heard" and that "one of these other *vus* would explain succinctly the baffling phenomenon of which he had been both a witness and a part." Another possibility is what the chaplain considers: that "it was even possible that none of what he thought had taken place, really had taken place, that he was dealing with an aberration of memory rather than of perception, that he never really had thought he had seen what he now thought he once did think he had seen, that his impression now that he once had thought so was merely the illusion of an illusion."

We all want to believe that our perceptions are reliable. We want to believe that our experiences have meaning. We want to trust that our explanations of what we experience make sense. To consider the possibility that we live our lives in a state of perceptual error—that our experiences are merely "the illusion of an illusion"—is not just disturbing but terrifying. It's as terrifying as the possibility that the ground we stand on isn't solid: that we could break through the surface at any moment and tumble into the void.

AS I THINK THROUGH ALL THESE ISSUES, what should I make of my early, inexplicable, lifelong obsession with the lute and its literature? More even than the Great War, the lute is the durable object of my strongest *déjà vu* experience. More than just *vu*—also *écouté, joué, aimé.* Even seeing a photo of a lute at age seven prompted an immediate, almost overwhelming sense of recognition and longing. Why? I had no idea at the time. Over sixty years later, I still have no idea. The sense of connection, however, the sense of belonging, lingers.

Responding to this experience, I could easily tell myself, "Your sense of recognition makes no sense, so by definition it's nonsense. What you experienced is just an aberration of memory—the illusion of an illusion." Or I could tell myself, "Your sense of recognition makes complete sense. It's a glimpse of a past lifetime, one in which you had some kind of involvement with the lute and its music. This prior lifetime surfaced into your present-day consciousness." The temptation to force clarity on this situation is powerful and constant, yet I still can't fully accept either of these explanations. I can't shed either of my longstanding epistemological approaches—being simultaneously skeptical and open-minded. I question everything yet won't rule out anything. Like Marlow in Joseph Conrad's *Heart of Darkness,* I am prone toward inconclusive experiences. Yet like Wordsworth, I sense intimations of immortality. I don't want to force superstructures of explanation on my experiences, or on others', just to avoid the discomfort of uncertainty.

Ultimately, I agree with a passage in a brief book by Gilbert Murray, an early-twentieth-century British scholar of ancient religions. Murray's remarks remain one of the best summaries I know regarding the issue of balancing rational and intuitive forms of inquiry:

As far as knowledge and conscious reason will go, we should follow resolutely their austere guidance. When they cease, as cease they must, we must use as best we can those fainter powers of apprehension and surmise and sensitive¬ness by which, after all, most high truth has been reached, as well as most high art and poetry: careful always really to seek for truth and not for our own emotional satisfaction; careful not to neglect the real needs of men and women through basing our life on dreams; and remembering above all to walk gently in a world where the lights are dim and the very stars wander. [24]

9/14

History is a nightmare
from which I am trying to awake.

—James Joyce, *Ulysses*

I'm back in the Land of the Living now after a night in Hell," I wrote to a friend the morning after, "truly one of the most bizarre, appalling, and moving experiences of my life." The night in question had begun on the evening of Friday, September 14, 2001, and had ended before dawn on the 15th. This was the night I spent as a volunteer EMT when the Maplewood (N.J.) First Aid Squad contributed a duty crew to emergency services present at the World Trade Center three days after the 9/11 attacks. To my surprise, the shift had proved uneventful, so my referring to it as "a night in Hell" was melodramatic and self-indulgent. I had visited a hellish landscape, however, and felt deeply shaken by the experience. To this same friend I wrote that my shift at the WTC had been "one I find difficult to think about without emotionally imploding, one I've managed to talk about only once so far, and then only blurtingly and haltingly. In many ways, nothing happened. At the same time, just being there hit hard on so many levels, and in such complex and contradictory ways, that I'm still reeling and struggling to sort it all out."

One day later, I attempted to record my experience at the WTC while the sights, sounds, smells, and other impressions were still fresh; and, to the degree possible at the time, to make sense of what I witnessed. Quoting now at length and almost verbatim, correcting only typos and unclear phrasings, here's what I wrote.

I. NOTES FROM GROUND ZERO

ON FRIDAY, AT AROUND 1:45 P.M., Maureen Power, the Maplewood First Aid Squad's lieutenant, left a message on our phone machine to determine my availability for a crew that would provide emergency medical services in the WTC area. Edith and I sized up the situation and decided that it would work out for me to take part. We both felt ambivalent about this decision, and during my absence that evening Edith felt still more so, but overall we concluded that I could contribute some time now with less disruption to our family than if I had gone in earlier this week or if I went in later. I personally felt that I should participate in the effort at some point, and that doing so now would work as well as anything. The weather was pretty good, too, and the previous night's heavy rain had apparently cleared the air to some degree in Lower Manhattan. That was a real plus—I had worried a lot about the toxic smoke down there. So, given the auspicious circumstances, I called Maureen back and said I would go. Maureen asked me to show up in about half an hour.

Shortly after I reached the Maplewood squad house, Maureen and I headed off to Newark in an ambulance driven by Scott Kalick, one of my Wednesday night shift buddies. The reason for going to Newark was to join a convoy of other crews that would enter NYC together. Also, we got a briefing at Rutgers University in Newark, which included a request to stock up on medical supplies, clean clothes (socks, underwear, etc.), and food/beverages that we would drop off for the crews doing extrication and excavation at the WTC site. The campus building we visited teemed with activity. Dozens of companies and nonprofit agencies have donated *matériel* of various sorts for this recovery effort. Basically we just grabbed whatever we thought we could find useful—band aids, gauze pads,

Visine, face masks, gloves—and loaded everything into the ambulance. I felt somewhat odd about this phase, as I couldn't quite imagine how and where we would disburse all this stuff while attempting to do EMS [emergency medical services] in the field. The sheer quantity of supplies got obstructive quickly. But those were our instructions, and we assumed that they bore some connection to reality. Another odd aspect of the situation was the relentless effort by volunteers at Rutgers to ply us with food. Hot food, cold food, junk food. . . (Were they fattening us up for the slaughter. . . ?!) Despite my usual healthy appetite I didn't feel much like eating, as I worried that doing so might not be wise if our work included some of the gruesome tasks that we believed we might be asked to perform.

Around 3:15, an EMS supervisor rounded up all ten participating crews and gave us a brief speech. The supervisor's emphasis was, predictably, on safety: step carefully, move slowly, and think constantly about what you're doing. He also said, "You'll be seeing things you wish you'd never have seen," and he urged us to support each other and stay in contact with field supervisors at all times. All very sobering. Then a minister came out and gave another speech, thanking us for our efforts and offering a prayer that focused on unity, serving others, and—nice touch—staying out of danger. His words moved me and to some degree unnerved me. Then we headed off.

Our convoy drove through Newark and some of the neighboring cities. Police blocked traffic all the way. We were a disruptive, noisy procession, with sirens blaring, but we went ahead without any mishap. Traffic all along proved to be heavily congested; I'm sure our passage made matters far worse. About halfway to the entrance to the Holland Tunnel, our crew had an annoying mishap: our siren died. This failure of equipment wasn't a disaster, but it wasn't a good thing, either, and it seemed inauspicious. After all, we didn't know what we would be doing for the next 12-18 hours, and an ambulance without a siren in NYC isn't in good shape. But we couldn't do anything about the problem. We just proceeded.

It was strange and eerie to enter the Holland Tunnel without the usual crush of congestion. The only vehicles present at that time were the vehicles in our convoy. We drove through and arrived in Manhattan about ten minutes later. Then the strangeness continued: the neighborhoods below Canal Street are closed to normal traffic, so that the only other cars and trucks we saw were fire department and police vehicles, NYC sanitation vehicles, and National Guard trucks of various sorts. Manhattan appeared to be an occupied city. The four of us in our crew—Maureen, 22; Scott Kalick, 49; Kier Bowers, 35; and I, the grand old man of the crew at 51—talked excitedly and nervously about how "this was it." We were on our way into what had been labeled the Hot Zone and perhaps all the way to Ground Zero.

Yet our convoy then turned right instead of left, heading north instead of south, and drove a couple of miles to a place called Chelsea Piers, which is a recreation area (driving range, gym, marina, etc.) right on the Hudson River. There we looped through the neighborhood and parked on West 17th Street in a queue of about fifteen other ambulances.

What followed between around 4:00 and 7:00 was a classic example of hurry-up-and-wait. Although we checked in with a supervising medic, we couldn't get a clear sense of how long we would be there before we got to do something. Some of the crews we chatted with had been waiting right there since seven that morning! The gloomy thought occurred to us that we might end up cooling our heels there all night, then get ordered home. When the four of us discussed the situation, we all felt frustrated. We couldn't do much about it, however, and so we figured we would just try to stay patient and take events as they happened. We soon learned a little more about our mission, however: we would be assigned to Advanced Life Support (ALS) medics (we are Basic Life Support emergency medical technicians, or BLS EMTs). The medics would answer medical or trauma calls that we would assist. That seemed fair enough. Yet even this seemingly important role was good news/bad news. It would be great to support an ALS team; on the other hand, we might get assigned elsewhere in Manhattan—some neighborhood uptown, perhaps—and thus never get near the WTC area at all. All of us felt pretty mixed about what we would be doing.

Soon we met the medics. They were a two-person crew based at University Hospital in Hackensack, N.J. The man, Don, seemed affable and pretty open to our presence. The woman, Paige, struck me as depressed, withdrawn, and unfriendly. I chalked up her attitude to stress and fatigue at the time. Later, I started to wonder if she might be suffering from something more serious, perhaps post-traumatic stress syndrome, which is common among career medics. I couldn't tell one way or the other. In any case, her manner didn't seem important at the time and didn't really cause any problems later.

The hours we spent at Chelsea Piers weren't a bad situation except for our eagerness to get going. A large area at the Piers— big as a single-floor parking garage—housed 50-75 volunteers who were amassing supplies for rescue effort personnel. They had stacked huge quantities of food, beverages, supplies, and clothing that they then invited us to take. Some of these people (mostly twenty- and thirty-something New Yorkers) were earnest about having us accept what they offered. Long tables of food had been set up with trays of lasagna, ziti, chicken parmesan, and other hot dishes, as well as salad, macaroni and cheese, and desserts. I also saw piles of cookies, chips, bagels, brownies, and all sorts of other stuff. Young women plied us with any kind of food they had available. They also urged us to stock up on packaged foods. Everything was free. The same held true for clothing, including sweaters, jackets, T-shirts, even underwear. Kier and I felt concerned about how chilly the air had gotten even since our arrival, so we took several extra layers. We also walked off with three or four raincoats.

The whole place had a festive, energetic atmosphere. More and more volunteers showed up over the next few hours. Piles of food, beverages, and other goods arrived in panel trucks. At one point I even saw National Guardsmen unloading pallets of dog food. *(Dog food!)* Somehow the scene at Chelsea Piers made this phase of the disaster seem as much a picnic as an emergency.

Then, abruptly at seven, we received word that we would be moving out shortly. We tracked down Don and Paige, got our equipment ready, and soon joined a southbound convoy.

We felt both excited and anxious to be en route to what we perceived as our goal. The three of us Maplewood crew members in the back of the rig talked animatedly about what we expected of the shift. Scott drove. Don sat up front with Scott. Paige, the dour medic with us, listened without much comment and occasionally teased us about our naiveté, or else made veiled remarks about what we would encounter. I realize that many medics have seen so much action that they've become thick-skinned, and many have a decidedly dark sense of humor, but this woman's gloomy attitude started to weigh on me. Once again, however, there wasn't anything to be done about it. Maureen, Kier, and I just looked out the windows to see the sights around us, and we talked about what we saw and what we thought about the whole scene, and I, at least, tried to ignore Paige as much as possible.

I should mention that off and on that afternoon, the other Maplewood EMTs and I had discussed our present situation and our reasons for taking part. The specific question was why we felt so driven to volunteer our time and effort in the city—specifically, why we wanted so much to get posted at the WTC. All of us felt ambivalent about the situation. As we kicked this topic around, however, we came up with a general sense of why we were there. I can speak only for myself, but some of the others expressed similar feelings. There was no single reason, just a jumble of reactions. One was a genuine desire to Do Something. We wanted to make a difference, if possible, to the people who had suffered this calamity. Another reason was a *misguided* desire to Do Something—that is, an effort to make a contribution that might, in fact, not be so helpful. The comparison I would make is to the surge in blood donations following the WTC disaster. New York City doesn't need 600,000 pints of blood right now. The hospitals need blood for the long haul, but a glut of donors is more of a problem than a solution. Perhaps we EMTs ran a similar risk by offering services that were now overly abundant. Yet another reason was that we wanted to be part of a major historical event. Finally, we all admitted to an element of voyeurism. We just wanted to see what had happened. These weren't necessarily the right motives, or pretty motives. . . Still, I guess it's better to 'fess up than to pretend otherwise.

We now plodded along on the West Side Highway, moving at perhaps five to ten miles per hour in a dense column of ambulances, police cars, and a few fire trucks, with some huge empty cargo trucks thrown in for good measure. I found it difficult to see much around us. The rig's side door has a small window, but it's hard to see out through it, and Paige ordered me not to open the slider. Perhaps she had good reason: we could already smell the acrid odors of the WTC fires. By looking through the passageway that connects the patient compartment to the front of the vehicle, we could see ahead occasionally and spot the massive slant of smoke—now illuminated by lamps to a bright white—and we could also see the silhouettes of some buildings and some sort of arch-like bridge in the eerie light. Then we took a couple of turns—left, then right—and headed south to circumvent the WTC area.

The first real shocks came as we drove down Broadway. At the intersections with Dey and Cortlandt Streets, we caught two views of the towers' wreckage: a three- or four-story piece of the south building's skeletal facade, then, one block further down, another enormous shred of metal, this one a massive parallelogram, perhaps four stories tall, pointing straight up. Both views were backlit by dazzling spotlights. Smoke, shifting behind and in front of them, intensified the sinister mood. The scenes also revealed great numbers of workers and pieces of heavy equipment—cranes and claw-like machines—near the wreckage. We saw incongruous other sights, too, such as a cluster of three Franciscan monks in their brown robes standing on a street corner staring at the workers and machinery. Another odd religious touch: we passed Trinity Church, a New York landmark that's beautiful in its own right and famous for having the oldest cemetery in the city. Edith had been worried about reports of the cemetery's destruction, as she is fond of this peaceful place and its history. From what I could see, the church is largely intact and the cemetery isn't destroyed, at least not on the east and south sides of the church. But it felt strange to look across the gravestones toward the ruins beyond.

Within a few minutes we proceeded down Broadway, then ended up at the corner of West and Battery Streets. This is right along the river at almost the farthest-south point in Manhattan. We parked the rig and got out. Seven or eight other rigs had parked nearby. At this point it was a relief to get out of the crowded patient compartment, but I felt mixed about what would happen next—concerned about how long we would be there and keyed up simply to be in such a strange and eerie place. The view up West Street revealed a dark corridor with abandoned buildings on both sides, a roadway crowded with construction vehicles, and a brilliantly illuminated work site overhung with a sky-high slant of white smoke. I could see vast cranes, dangling cables, and the indistinct heap of WTC rubble. The air was acrid but not unbearable. Fortunately, the wind had shifted to the east, taking much of the smoke away from us. We stood around for a while adjusting our equipment—face masks, goggles, and hard hats—while awaiting word of what to do.

Apparently the plan was for us simply to wait there until called to provide medical care to injured or sick workers. The likelihood of treating a survivor of the WTC collapse itself was small at best. Almost four days after the disaster, the odds of finding survivors had diminished greatly. The far greater chance was that we would be treating a site worker who had cut himself on torn metal, twisted his ankle, gotten grit in his eyes, or suffered smoke inhalation. In a more extreme scenario, we might be treating someone who had suffered more serious trauma—a fall into the wreckage, perhaps—or perhaps a work-induced cardiac problem. Whatever my personal unease toward Paige, I felt confident that she and Don would be proficient medics. I felt in good hands at least in that sense, which is significant, given the difficulty of caring for severely ill or injured patients anyway, all the more so in unfamiliar surroundings. Also, I felt reassured that we Maplewoodians would be allowed—in fact, ordered—to stay together as a group; there had been some speculation about our ending up mixed in with another squad. Perhaps most intensely, I felt relieved that we wouldn't end up assigned to one of the bucket brigades extricating body parts from the wreckage. I've been around severely injured people before in my hospital jobs, as well as dead bodies, and I've witnessed all sorts of trauma, including dismemberment, but I had little interest in being part of the extrication detail four days after the disaster. This option now seemed out of the question.

What followed was about six hours of waiting and wandering. We did not have any EMS calls. As far as I was concerned, our idleness was entirely a good thing, as it meant that none of the workers at the WTC site had suffered any distress serious enough to require our attention. My understanding is that many workers at Ground Zero suffer minor accidents, and many experience respiratory irritation and eye irritation from the smoke, but those people all end up taken care of by BLS crews. Since we were an ALS crew, we wouldn't attend to those relatively smaller emergencies. The result: we ended up free alternately to stay in the ambulance and to wander in the area. One of the rules meant that at least one EMT had to stay with the rig at all times. We could be in radio or cell-phone contact with each other, however, so the others could prowl about and see the sights.

All told, I took three walks up to Ground Zero that night. The first didn't go very far, as we stopped short of a cordon manned by National Guardsman. They were cordial but firm about not letting us through. On the two later walks, however, we talked with the guards, presented our squad i.d. cards, and got waved through. This allowed us to go right up to the final barrier at Ground Zero, which NYC police are staffing and which only construction workers, police officers, FBI agents, and a few others can pass. Still, we got really close. I would say we were within about thirty yards of the close edge of the rubble and about fifty yards of the North Tower heap that rises to maybe five stories above the ground.

The sight is difficult to describe. In recent days, many journalists have invoked Dante and Hieronymus Bosch in attempting to write about the WTC site. These comparisons sound like clichés but are impossible to avoid. There's something truly hellish about the site—its strange mix of starkness and complexity; the harshness of the light; the depth of the shadows; the pieces of wreckage angling every which way; the blank flat, pale, gray-tan silt covering every surface; the fires burning here and there, some of them as large as rooms yet tiny compared to the heap itself; the palls of bone-white smoke angling off the heap; the sheer *deadness* of the whole mass. Add to that two or three hundred tiny figures, each with a tiny white, yellow, orange or blue hardhat, all these tiny bodies swarming together on the lower surface of the wreckage and it's almost impossible not to perceive the scene as unearthly, sinister, infernal. All the while there's horrendous noise, with huge trucks coming and going, heavy machinery picking up and dropping girders and tangles of wreckage, jack hammers pounding, and front loaders grinding around in the dirt carrying supplies. The intense klieg lights intensified the air of unreality, drenching the whole scene with almost blinding white light. At Ground Zero, other buildings rise all around, many of them not visibly damaged, but since they're entirely dark, they have a stony, tomb-like appearance rather than one that seems part of the living world. Underfoot is a strange, pale brown slimy mud, a mix of dirt, pulverized concrete, and ashes.

I watched this sight for a long time, both during the first walk and the second, and felt both drawn to keep watching and eager to leave. What made it bearable was the presence of so many people clearly intent on doing what they came here to do: police officers, firefighters, FBI agents, construction workers, and National Guardsman. Despite all the variety of their roles and appearances, there was an odd unity to these people. All had come here to join the same effort. It's easy to rattle on about the virtues of this communitarian effort, but it was a stirring sight, too, and greatly admirable for what it says about all these workers' generosity of spirit. (We learned earlier of crews that had driven from as far away as Maine, Texas, and North Carolina just to offer their services.) Still, the place itself offers such a chilling vision that I personally felt as much repulsion as attraction; after watching for a while, I would quickly feel the urge to get away.

One of the most appalling sights was a heap of wrecked vehicles about half a block from Ground Zero. This heap rose about two stories tall and must have been at least half a hundred feet long and perhaps fifty feet wide. My guess is that all the wreckage there had been pulled away from the WTC area by heavy-equipment operators and stored there for the time being. Among the vehicles I saw were at least a dozen cars, some of them smashed almost flat, others twisted; a New York Fire Department ladder truck that had been twisted almost a full quarter turn, so that the front end was upright but the back end was on its side; and two ambulances, one of them with the patient compartment ripped in half, the other flattened from side to side. I have no idea how many vehicles rested in the heap. My guess is perhaps thirty or forty. Later, when we ventured elsewhere, I saw another stack of cars, many of them flattened, including a yellow taxi cab that looked about two feet tall from roof to floor.

Other strange touches:

Paper everywhere—pages of spreadsheets, calendar pages, pages of reports, pages of computer printouts, pages of hard copy e-mail, pages and pages and pages. Some were shredded to confetti, but most were intact, lying on the ground but also plastered against buildings, matted against chain link fences, clogging the railing along the deck of what used to be the South Tower, caught up the branches of trees, scattered everywhere.

Belongings: a busted open suitcase; men's clothing—socks, pants, a sports jacket; an umbrella; a pair of running shoes.

Wreckage in odd places: stuck in the fire escape of an old building along Greenwich Street, a fifteen-foot length of steel beam.

Graffiti: right along the windows at the base of the South Tower—the panes inexplicably unbroken—I saw "Kilroy Was Here"-type comments scrawled in the dust. "South Amboy Rescue Squad." "Little Falls First Aid." "FDNY Ladder No. 134." Dozens of others, too, crowded each other into illegibility. Some cries-of-the heart as well: "God Bless America!!!" and "United We Stand."

We retreated to our ambulance, chatted with other crews, and rested a while. The two medics showed up for a while and sat up front. Scott spent some of his time outside talking with EMTs from East Hanover, N.J. Maureen, Kier, and I hung out inside the rig, each of us finding a place to rest on the stretcher, the side bench, or the floor. We talked off and on, mostly about what had seen; Maureen made calls to her family and friends;

I dozed briefly. During this time the wind must have shifted, for the air quality deteriorated and the acrid smell intensified. I started to wonder if our face masks—intended to filter particulate matter, not fumes—would really prove adequate. My nasal passages, throat, trachea, and lungs started to hurt more than before. I also worried that my beard was compromising the mask's efficiency, since facial hair would let bad air to slip around. When I would take off the mask, however, I would notice at once how much worse the air smelled, so the filter must have been making a big difference after all. I kept the mask on throughout most of the remaining time we spent there.

Somewhat after 2:30, we decided to go for another walk. This time Maureen, Kier, Scott, and I hung out at the Ground Zero final barricade for a while, but then, as a group, we ventured east on Liberty Street, worked our way around a lot of workers cutting fallen beams apart with acetylene torches, and turned left onto Greenwich Street. There we confronted a sight that was in many ways the most horrific of the whole night. This was the ruins of the South Tower. First of all, we managed to get much closer to the rubble than had done earlier, perhaps twenty yards or so. Second, we got a closer view of the workers sifting through the wreckage. The whole area was, in fact, teeming with workers. We had arrived at a change of shift: eighty or a hundred workers, equipped with hard hats and respirators and clad in coveralls (or, in some cases, pale blue Tyvek biohazard outfits), walked out of the excavation site; another large phalanx of workers marched in. Their actions seemed matter-of-fact, their demeanor tired but not as bone-weary as I had heard from news accounts. To some degree they looked little different from a contingent of miners leaving after a long day's work while another contingent showed up for the next shift. Among this crowd I also saw dozens of police officers, fire fighters, FBI agents, and others of uncertain identity. We were the only EMTs present. We stood near a long cargo truck and watched a work crew lower a thirty- or forty-foot length of twisted steel beam into place by means of a crane. On our left stood several dozen rows of stacked ten-gallon plastic buckets, each stack about ten or fifteen buckets deep. (These are the buckets used for collecting body parts.) At a few dozen yards' distance, teams of people picked through the debris. A vast pile of rubble—beams jutting out of its surface—rose to our left. (If I had wanted to, I could have walked just ten or fifteen feet and touched the nearest edge of this pile. There must have been bodies within a few yards of us.) Palls of smoke rose from the heap ahead of us. Somehow the most frightening sight, however, was the backdrop to this scene: a triangle of WTC facade rising at least five or six stories straight ahead, its vast metal ribs resembling part of the torn ribcage of a massive beast. The smoke shifted now and then, fully revealing this piece of skeleton at times, then shrouding it, then revealing it again, a taunting, threatening apparition.

What struck me just then was that if there's ever a nuclear war, these sights will be what the world will look like. We'll have a world in which life diminishes almost to nothing and death becomes almost everything, in which what little remains of life consists of survivors' efforts to pick through the ruins.

We didn't have much to do but stare. Staring felt helpless, almost pointless, and in some ways pitiful, but it seemed important anyway. It's easy to invoke the role of bearing witness; it's tempting to find solace in it; and it's risky to believe that doing so is a sufficient response. At the same time, I still think there's a need to take the opportunity, to stare, and to attempt to make sense of what we see. So that's what we did. The four of us stayed at the South Tower site for about twenty minutes, watched, handed out some face masks to personnel who didn't have any, then retreated. It seemed time to clear out. We also wondered—I did, anyway—about the possibility of our being ordered to leave, since we didn't really have any specific role right there at the time. Anyway, we left. We retraced our steps, walked down West Street to our ambulance, and hunkered down again.

Shortly after that—around 3 a.m.—central command dismissed us. Our crew and the two medics left the Battery Park area, drove north, and headed for Chelsea Piers. On the way out we saw more clusters of soldiers, more convoys of rescue and construction vehicles, and more National Guard transport units. Their number diminished as we passed Canal Street, however, and we soon started seeing more normal sights. Korean produce stores. All-night delis. Newsstands. Clusters of young people hanging out on street corners. People walking their dogs. This being New York City, lots of folks were out and about even at three a.m. What struck me, though, was how normal these sights seemed—how blessedly *ordinary*. A young woman rollerblading on the avenue. Some boys eating pizza in front of an Italian joint. A couple out for a walk. A woman listening to music or news on a Walkman. I found these sights astonishing, moving, and reassuring, for they refuted the state of mind I had entered while at the WTC—that life had withered away during our time in the ruins.

Just a short while later, once had reached Chelsea Piers and helped Paige and Don move their equipment out of our rig and load it onto their own, the four members of our crew headed out of New York. Even at three a.m. we saw people along the West Side Highway who cheered us and waved their hand-lettered signs ("We Love You," "Thanks for Your Support!" "God Bless the U.S.!!!" "Thank You!!!!") as we passed. Some Guardsman checked our documents and waved us on. One last touch that would stun anyone accustomed to New York City traffic: we were only vehicle in whole length of the Holland Tunnel.

II. THE 9/14 CATECHISM;
OR, WHAT PEOPLE HAVE ASKED ME

Q: SO, HOW DID YOU FEEL ABOUT ALL THAT?

A: How do you *think* I felt? I was exhausted, unnerved, and scared. My family and I lived eighteen miles from lower Manhattan. For many days after the attacks—for months, actually—neither we nor anyone else had any idea what might happen next. Seeing the scope of the damage up close on September 14th made it impossible not to worry.

Q: Why is your account so unemotional?

A: We were too busy staying alert to feel most emotions. Even at the time my fellow-EMTs and I admitted to one another that we felt depressed about the attacks and scared about being present at The Pile. But we focused on paying attention on what was happening around us and on being ready to offer assistance is anyone among the personnel on site got injured or sick. This approach is typical of what I had experienced throughout my years of EMS work, as well as during my ten years of working in hospitals. Some degree of disengagement goes with the role. Some degree of dissociation, even. I'm not saying that this reaction lacks drawbacks, but it's a standard experience for EMTs, emergency department staffers, firefighters, police, and soldiers.

Q: Is it true that nothing much happened after 9/11?

A: The answer to that question depends on what you mean by "nothing," "much," and "happened." First of all, someone in New Jersey began mailing anthrax-tainted letters starting a week after the 9/11 attacks. Five deaths resulted, as well as seventeen non-fatal injuries. One of the affected post offices was just five miles from our town. While it now appears that the anthrax incidents resulted from domestic terrorism, not from *jihadi* actions, the situation wasn't clear as it unfolded. (Many months later, investigations clarified that the anthrax attacks were unrelated to al-Qaeda or other *jihadi* groups, but it's still not clear who might have been the perpetrators.) Then, on November 12th, American Airlines flight 587 crashed off Queens, New York, prompting fears that terrorists had caused the accident. 260 people died. I was skeptical even at the time that these incidents were necessarily related to the 9/11 attacks, but, like everyone else, I couldn't help but wonder. Investigations into the accident concluded much later that the plane crashed as a result of combined pilot error and equipment failure, but what I witnessed on the night of September 14th certainly made it easy to feel paranoid about any number of incidents that took place during 2001. At least in the New York metro area, this paranoia didn't ease for several years.

Q: What were you expecting?

A: Not any specific event. I was just hedging my bets. First off, my wife and I worried, like many or most Americans at the time, about a second wave of attacks. This concern prompted Edith and me to stockpile food, water, and other supplies in case we had to hunker down. Even absent actual attacks, we figured that the widespread fear of attacks, especially if fear led to outright panic, could have made the metro area dangerous. It doesn't take a real attack to cause social upheaval. For this reason, we prepared for trouble. We decided, among other things, that we might have to evacuate to New England, where a friend offered to take us in.

Q: Wasn't that rather alarmist?

A: Again, it depends on what your use of the word means. What constitutes being "alarmist"? In October, the regional Office of Emergency Management alerted all the Tri-state EMT squads, including ours in Maplewood, N.J., of information concerning a plausible threat to the New York area. A *jihadi* in detention at the time claimed that members of his cell had smuggled a "dirty bomb" into Manhattan. Later, this claim proved to be bogus. But the possibility that someone might detonate a weapon of this sort, killing hundreds or thousands of people and rendering much of the city uninhabitable, wasn't something I felt ready to brush off. I would call my concern *alarmed,* not *alarmist.*

Q: And then?

A: Nothing much happened on a local level. But the United States invaded Afghanistan, achieved some initial victories, then eventually bogged down in a quagmire that has continued for almost two decades so far. In 2003, the Bush administration used the 9/11 attacks as a pretext for invading Iraq, overthrew Saddam Hussein's regime, established a nominally democratic government, but also triggered a sectarian conflict that continues in Iraq to this day and that spread to neighboring countries, destabilized the Middle East overall, gave rise to the Syrian civil war, and greatly increased Iran's influence in the area.

Q: How did the aftermath of the EMT shift affect you personally?

A: Nothing dramatic happened, but the overall situation wasn't positive. Most of the effects were psychological. Some were physical, however. Although I spent less than eight hours on duty at the WTC site, I coughed for weeks afterwards. I kept smelling an acrid, foul odor for a long time, too, as if particulates or chemicals had embedded themselves in my respiratory system. When I commented about the coughing and the smell to a local friend—our town's fire chief at the time—he said, "Well, you got yourself a snoot full of smoke." True. But more than just smoke. Studies undertaken after the attacks indicate that the WTC site's air contained particles of cement, steel, gypsum (from drywall), building materials, cellulose (from paper), fiberglas (from insulation), glass particles, human tissues and hair, and synthetic materials (from cubicles and rugs), as well as vaporized jet fuel, benzene, and as many as perhaps two or three hundred other toxic chemicals. Few of the personnel present in the aftermath wore respirators. My fellow squad members and I used only N-95 masks—the kind you might use during a basement cleanup or a woodworking project—as protection. It's not surprising that we hacked for months from what was later dubbed "the World Trade Center cough." In 2003, after many bouts of bronchitis, my physician ordered me to undergo a full pulmonary workup to see if I'd suffered significant damage. The results of diagnostic tests were reassuring. But the pulmonologist who reviewed the data told me, "We've never studied patients exposed to a mix of so many chemicals, so we don't really know what the long-term outcome will be."

Q: Were there any other aftereffects?

A: Lots of nightmares and periodic flashbacks. That being said, I'm aware that I got off easy in every possible way. I was present at the site for only a single shift, and I didn't go through the hardships that so many personnel did during their much longer and more numerous rotations into the site. I didn't witness the horrific sights that so many first responders and iron workers did. Yet the hours I spent there definitely got under my skin. I still think about that night. In addition, my shift created some marital tensions. My wife had given me her go-ahead to volunteer for that shift, but she didn't really want me to participate. The fact that even my ordinary shifts on the Maplewood squad entailed more risk day after day is probably beside the point.

Q: What else?

A: It's impossible to have that kind of experience without it darkening one's mood about everything. The 9/11 attacks and their consequences were an utter waste. The attacks accomplished nothing positive. In addition to killing 2,996 people on September 11th (in Manhattan, Washington, D.C., and in Shanksville, Pennsylvania), the attacks led to two ill-considered, destructive wars that have done nothing to improve the world—that have, in fact, killed at least half a million people and have made the world a far more dangerous place. The events that took place on 9/11, as well events in the aftermath, seem altogether pointless.

Q: So, what do you feel that you yourself accomplished that night?

A: Not much. Maybe nothing.

III. FOG

I HAD ALWAYS DISLIKED THE TOWERS. Ever since moving to the New York area in 1982, I considered them a soulless monument to corporate arrogance. Nothing about them drew me forth. I had gone inside the buildings only twice: first, during the early 1990's, when my wife's English cousin James took us for drinks at Windows on the World, the WTC's 106th-floor restaurant; and a few years later, when Edith and I hosted out-of-town visitors for an excursion to the observation deck. Although I found both events memorable because of the impressive 360-degree panoramas that the tower provided—during the first visit, a limitless sea of lights; during the second, an essentially aerial view of the New York megalopolis as far as the eye could see—neither occasion prompted me to feel any affection for the World Trade Center itself.

However, I had one other experience of the towers that lingers in my memory. One early-winter evening during the late 1980's, during my brief employment as the staff writer for a Midtown engineering firm, I went down to the World Trade Center after work. I can't recall why I happened to be in Lower Manhattan. I might have attended a meeting somewhere in the area, or I may have been present following an art class I took in Soho for several months. In any case, I found myself at the WTC plaza around dusk in rainy weather. Darkness had fallen. A lid of heavy clouds had descended on the city. I strayed onto the plaza, probably looking for the subway entrance as I worked my way back to Brooklyn. The plaza itself was mostly empty as other people headed home after work. I looked upward to see an unnerving sight. The towers, fully illuminated from the ground level all the way up to the 40th or 50th stories, started to diminish beyond that, kept fading floor by floor, then vanished altogether into fog.

Pyrocopia

After Steve and I placed the bomb on that clear, calm summer evening in 1966, we left the schoolyard, strolled across the baseball field, crossed Iowa Avenue, moseyed a half-block down Adams Street, walked into Steve's backyard, and seated ourselves in the porch swing facing the lawn. The fuse we had lit, red and rope-like, burned at a rate of one inch per second. Its ten-foot length had given us two minutes of escape time, enough for us to depart from the John J. Cory Elementary School grounds at a leisurely pace that wouldn't draw attention. We now sat far away from our handiwork. The bomb, meanwhile, resting atop the fifteen-foot shaft of the ring set in the playground, awaited the flame like a prisoner just moments before his execution. The bomb was a roll of toilet paper plugged at each end with one-inch-thick slices of wood cut from a dowel. Into one of the plugs Steve and I had drilled a hole big enough to insert the fuse. The charge inside the roll was a cup of homemade black powder. We were pleased with our handiwork. At age sixteen, we were both straight-A students, compliant at school, cooperative at home—"good boys." Neither of us resembled any kind of juvenile delinquent. We didn't cause even the most harmless sorts of trouble at school or anywhere else. On the contrary, our teachers respected us and considered us gifted students. Our parents loved us, trusted us, and gave us almost total leeway to do as we pleased during the mid-1960's era of American culture that allowed kids to play with only minimal supervision and let teens go about their activities unattended. Having now laid the groundwork for a boyish prank, Steve and I sat on the Fedders' porch swing and waited.

A long time passed. Two minutes? At least. Why did we hear only the ordinary sounds of a summer night in Denver—the dialogue from a neighbor's TV, the music from a second neighbor's stereo, the drone from a lawn mower down the block? Perhaps the fuse had gone out. Perhaps the bomb was a dud.

When the explosion reached us, the shock wave rattled windows in the houses around us and set every dog in the area barking. I had never heard a louder boom. I couldn't believe the force of it. Everywhere in the neighborhood Steve and I heard doors opening and people stepping outside. "What was *that?*" someone across the alley asked. Steve and I, shocked and amazed by the detonation's magnitude and by the neighbors' bewilderment, exchanged nervous glances and struggled to stifle our laughter—laughter that didn't express delight so much as astonishment and belated alarm at what we had perpetrated.

1. Good Boys

Even in the first few minutes after the bomb went off, I knew we had done something unusually dangerous and stupid. It's true that the summer evening was the kind when most families would be in their backyards chatting or else indoors watching TV; it's true as well that before setting up the bomb, Steve and I had scanned the schoolyard to confirm that nobody else was present or nearby; but it's also true that nothing would have prevented someone, most likely a child, from wandering over to the playground equipment after Steve and I had left. What if a boy or girl had decided to make one last climb up the jungle gym next to the rings? What if a child had chosen to take a spin on the rings themselves? Our toilet-paper bomb wouldn't have scattered shrapnel in the usual sense—pieces of metal—but even flying specks of cardboard or paper could have injured a kid's face or, worse yet, his or her eyes. The blast could have deafened a child. Up close, the shock wave could have blinded him or her. None of those scenarios escaped my imagination *after the explosion*. In prospect, however, the risk to others' health and wellbeing somehow hadn't occurred to us.

If we were such good boys, why did we perpetrate a crime— *breach of the peace* or *disturbing the peace,* if nothing else? Why, indeed, were we routinely building smaller bombs and all manner of fireworks in the Fedder family's garage? Why had Steve and I become so engrossed in such a dangerous hobby? Why did our efforts grow more and more complex, ambitious, and technically sophisticated? Why did our pyrotechnic projects become ever more powerful, more destructive, more potentially disastrous? It's true that we were "free-range kids" (to use the twenty-first-century terminology) and thus at liberty to choose and undertake our own activities, among them activities that would now be considered unacceptably dangerous. Even so, concocting pyrotechnic mixtures, including explosives, now seems beyond what almost all parents would have permitted even in that more lenient era.

Perhaps Steve and I got a pass because we were congenial, cooperative, well behaved, and less moody than most teenage boys. Our excellence in academic pursuits and our compliant behavior earned us respect and trust. That said, we were capable of clandestine mischief. Teenage boys have always done risky, dumb things. The adolescent brain is intellectually vibrant but ethically immature and often limited in its ability to grasp cause-effect relationships. Turbocharged by testosterone, the adolescent male brain, especially, often acts on impulse and with poor judgment. Boys have surely always engaged in shenanigans—whether St. Augustine's theft of pears in 349 or my theft of raspberries from Mrs. Evans down the block in 1957. During most of American history, the standard explanation for this phenomenon—more or less a blank check for low-grade troublemaking—has been simply "boys will be boys." That this motto has served to excuse egregious behavior now seems obvious. Until recently, however, the phrase generally explained and often absolved boys from many hazardous activities. Boys drove fast, climbed buildings, swam in flooded quarries, bungeed off bridges, and experimented with fireworks. I often wonder how my parents, both bohemian free-thinkers but nonetheless committed to ethical behavior, permitted the antics that I—along with my brothers and our friends—perpetrated. From the ages of around seven or eight on, we were allowed to play with only minimal supervision. We undertook projects that few or no American parents would permit today. Our early teen years offered even greater freedom. Steve and I constructed complex tree houses, dug holes up to nine feet deep, and rode off on our bicycles to explore the city and didn't come back home for hours. Our late-teen activities focused on driving into the Rockies to climb 13,000- and 14,000-foot peaks whose conditions often exceeded our mountaineering skills and experience. If that degree of freedom led to our making fireworks in the Fedders' garage during the mid-1960's, the pyrotechnic R&D project somehow wasn't outside the normal parameters.

II. Pyrocopia

Denver County, where both my own family and the Fedders lived, prohibited the sale of all fireworks. Just five blocks east of my family's house, however, Colorado Boulevard marked the border with Arapahoe County, where selling fireworks was legal. Despite the commercial ban, Denver didn't prohibit use of Class C products—"consumer fireworks intended for the general public." Kids in our neighborhood didn't have to go far to acquire the items we wanted—the items that I, too, was allowed to acquire starting at the age of seven or eight. My parents gave me some money each summer to purchase fireworks ahead of Independence Day. I awaited this holiday with an eagerness exceeded only by my anticipation of Christmas, and for a similar reason: not because of these holidays' core natures, whether patriotic or religious, but because they presented an opportunity to acquire exciting consumer goods. So, with five or six dollar bills crumpled in my pocket, I accompanied my father and my brothers for the brief ride up Mexico Avenue, across Colorado Boulevard, and into the promised land of pyrotechnics. There we found fireworks stands in many of the local stores' parking lots—flimsy little shacks thrown together from two-by-fours and plywood sheets, each vying for customers' attention with their bright red, white, and blue paint jobs. Most had huge signs across the top reading FIREWORKS or BEST FIREWORKS or ALL-AMERICAN FIREWORKS. The clerks behind the counters were local high-school boys who stood around chewing gum and looking bored while the customers sized up the merchandise. My brothers and I surveyed all the different options and struggled to make up our minds.

The goods? Fountains of many kinds: cones resembling miniature volcanoes, tube-like things mounted on little wooden bases, and big monsters, fat as Christmas candles, with names like Meteor Shower and Golden Cascade. Roman candles: torches guaranteed to spit out green, pink, yellow, orange, and red fireballs in a blast of sparks. Pinwheels—some no larger than the lid on a jam jar; others about as wide as a saucer; and still others, big as pie pans, designed to nail into a tree or a telephone pole to keep steady as they whirled. Bottle rockets, too, which I viewed as especially exciting. Little ones: skinny sticks with a tube and a wick at one end. Medium-sized rockets, too, each with a fatter tube, a thicker wick, and a stick two or three feet long. Big ones as well, with pointy plastic nose cones and real fins instead of sticks to stabilize them in flight. Other items: snakes, which created hideous black coils of ash as they burned; torpedoes, which made a loud bang when thrown down against the pavement; torches, which shot sparks and color into the air like fountains; and sparklers, of course, which my brothers and I held in contempt as suitable only for little kids. Firecrackers? No, even Arapahoe County banned the sale of explosives. By the ages of seven or eight, however, I already knew that these forbidden fruits weren't truly beyond reach. Jefferson County, west of Denver, was truly the pyrotechnic Garden of Eden.

I recall trembling with eagerness as I viewed the splendid array of incendiary merchandise. Facing the cornucopia before me—the *pyrocopia*—how could I pick out just a few dollars' worth? How could I narrow my choices when so many splendid fireworks sat displayed before me on the shelves? My brothers and I considered the options under our father's watchful gaze. At some point Dad would say, "Okay, it's time to make up your minds." I would continue staring, examining items that the counter guy handed over, picking and choosing, and gradually adding to the pile that accumulated before me. Then, as the clerk grew more and more impatient, I said, "Okay—*this* stuff." I surrendered my money. The transaction now complete, I dumped my stash of fireworks into a paper bag, carried the bag to our car, and, once my brothers finished their equivalent purchases, rode home.

During the week before Independence Day, I would repeatedly take out the bag, dump its contents onto my bed, and examine what I'd bought. This inventory inspired the same intense, warm anticipation I felt when examining my wrapped Christmas presents under the tree during the days leading up to that other, bigger holiday. Just looking at this arsenal delighted me. The bright colors! The wild designs—sparks, smoke, and flames! The odd warnings in half-intelligible English: *"Not light without parent in place."* These fireworks smelled bad, like rotten eggs or something worse. Even my excitement didn't blind me to the fact that they were dangerous. Now and then I heard reports of kids suffering injuries. One year my older brother, Rick, seared his right hand when an illicit firecracker exploded prematurely. I was appalled by the sight of the yellowish-gray blisters, greasy with ointment, on several of his fingers. News from the wider world alarmed me still more: a kid somewhere had gotten extensively burned, another kid blew off two fingers, a third got blinded by an explosion. These incidents made our parents' warnings plausible. They prompted my younger brother and me to comply with the rules. But the danger only added to fireworks' mystery and strangeness. Of course I would never be so stupid as to get hurt. I would covet and acquire these powerful devices, but I would honor them, too. I would be careful. For these and other reasons, the fountains, torches, and bottle rockets didn't scare me; they delighted me. They pulsed with energy. They promised spectacle and excitement. I could imagine the light and smoke and colored flames hiding inside, eager to burst forth, and the power I felt by owning them gave me a great sense of well-being.

What followed our acquisition of fireworks was the windup to the Fourth itself, an advent of sorts well ahead of the holiday's arrival. Throughout the neighborhood the whistles, shrieks, bangs, and booms started early in June and grew louder and more frequent. Most kids in the neighborhood, and especially the boys, set off fireworks each evening. A sulfurous pall wafted across the yards. Even by simply standing on our own lawn and looking above the trees I could see golden trails of sparks rise into the twilight. The cacophony and spectacle included not only the permissible devices but firecrackers too. Most of the bangs sounded like Black Cats, the most common of the explosive products. Neighbor kids acquired these by purchasing them in counties west of Denver. Not all families allowed their sons this special treat. (The pint-sized munitions experts of that era were almost always boys.) Parental bans didn't mean that boys with cautious parents had no access to otherwise restricted items, however; simply going over to a friend's house would allow easy access to the contraband. Black Cats were, in fact, traded and sold within a boyish underground economy. My brother Rick bought some from his pal Larry down the block. I was impressed and thrilled by my first sight of these firecrackers: inch-and-a-half-long tubes, black and white in design, connected in tidy chains by stringy paper wicks. They looked like the ammunition belts I'd seen in war movies. Setting off a batch of Black Cats was dramatic but short-lived and not interesting. More fun was disentangling the wicks and igniting the firecrackers one by one. This approach allowed much more amusement, including daredevil games: how long can you wait before tossing or flicking it away? Even riskier games involved launching Black Cats from slingshots. Burns were a constant threat. Later on I realized, however—realized with great excitement—that if I opened up enough firecrackers, I could amass enough powder to make something much more powerful. The results were not, however, the biggest eruption in my life at that time.

III. Family Explosions

What I remember is a desperate, protracted fight. A teenager's assault against an older male deteriorated into mortal combat. The teenager, lean but athletic at age seventeen, wrapped his hands around his opponent's throat and shoved both thumbs into his trachea. The older man, forty-seven years old, six-two in height, and strong, struggled to fight off the youth now throttling him. He grabbed the teenager by the shoulders, shook him hard, and, growing desperate, slammed him against the wall. Red-faced and desperate for breath, he couldn't overpower his assailant. All the while, three people watched helplessly from within the same room. One was a small fifty-one-year-old woman. The other two were boys: one thirteen, the other eleven years old. Terrified and bewildered, none of these witnesses to the struggle had any idea what to do. Join the battle? Hit the teenager with a book or lamp or shoe? Flee the room, run to a neighbor's house, and call the police? Lurching around the room and slamming into furniture, the combatants fought without either of them gaining the upper hand.

The older man was my father. The teenager was my older brother, Rick. The woman was my mother. Of the two boys watching, one was my younger brother, Dan; I was the other.

I don't recall what broke the standoff. Somehow the fighting stopped. The *mano-a-mano* ended in a draw. Either my dad succeeded in overpowering Rick, or else Rick reached an insight that killing his father wasn't a good idea after all. In any case, the combat came to a halt. It was, however, the worst and most dangerous upheaval in a crisis that had smoldered and periodically burst forth over a period of fourteen years.

My family had struggled with difficulties throughout the early 1960's. Although my mother and father had a strong marriage, and though they had always been loving, attentive parents, an aspect of our overall situation had gone sour. The core issue was my older brother, Rick. Born in early 1947 to a single mother, Rick had spent the first two and a half years of his life in a state-run orphanage. My parents, childless at the time and coping with issues of infertility, decided to adopt a baby. In that era, adoption did not yet require prospective parents to run the bureaucratic gauntlet that began evolving a few years later. My parents simply filled out several pages of paperwork, underwent a brief interview, and hosted a social worker for a single home visit. As an educated, well-employed couple—both were university professors—they were a shoe-in for approval. The process took shape quickly and auspiciously. On visiting the orphanage to select a baby, however, they found themselves mobbed by the toddlers and preschoolers living there. "Kids rushed over to us when we went into their playroom," my mother told me during my teens, "and they were clamoring for attention and hanging onto us—grabbing our legs and clinging to us. It was heartbreaking. The only playthings present were wooden blocks and some cardboard boxes. We learned later that the child-to-caregiver ratio was thirty to one. All the women could manage was keeping the kids fed and clean. The children got very little attention otherwise. They were starving for love." Visiting the orphanage in 1949, my parents faced the dilemma of picking out a child as they might have selected a puppy at a pet store. My mother said, "We had planned to adopt a baby. But when we saw all those desperate toddlers and school-age children, we decided to give one of the older kids a chance. We ended up choosing Rick." For an orphaned two-and-a-half-year-old accustomed to a stark institutional life, going off to live with a loving, middle-class couple must have been an ascent into paradise. The first year of Rick's adjustment went well.

During that same year, however, came a surprising twist in the family plot: late in the summer of 1949, my parents' infertility somehow eased. They conceived a child. I was born in April of 1950. All only-children experience shock upon the arrival of a new baby, so it's not surprising that Rick did, too. Yet he probably viewed me as an even less-welcome interloper than most siblings do. Almost immediately he started acting out. His behavior deteriorated during my infancy and early toddlerhood. Our younger brother, Dan, was born less than two years later. From then on, my biological brother and I were subject to what psychologists and social workers described later to my parents as unusually severe sibling rivalry. Rick pitted Dan and me against each other, mocked us continually, subjected us to other kinds of psychological abuse, and sometimes lashed out physically as well. The situation continued to deteriorate over the next several years. When Rick entered adolescence, his attitudes and behavior grew even worse. He caused trouble at school, shoplifted items from stores, stole money and possessions from the family, picked fights with local boys, lied to my parents about his activities, and grew more and more hostile and manipulative toward Dan and me.

During my boyhood and teen years, I couldn't understand my brother Rick's anger toward my parents. They had rescued him in late toddlerhood from the desolation of a state orphanage; they had nurtured and loved him; they had always treated him as the equal of their biological sons. Why, then, would he lash out with increasing frequency, intensity, and violence? Why would he even attack them physically—attack them almost to the point of homicide? His behavior made no sense. During my college years, however, I started to grasp the sources of Rick's paradoxical hostility. Reading articles by the Austrian-born psychiatrist René Spitz and, later, books by the British psychiatrist John Bowlby, I gained some insights into child development and, specifically, into aspects of developmental pathology. Dr. Spitz was a pioneer in researching the damage that children suffer when deprived of attention and affection, especially during babyhood and toddlerhood.[1] (Many of his studies focused on children in orphanages and the harm they suffered from institutionalization at formative stages of development.) Dr. Bowlby took his research many steps further, clarifying the nature of bonding and attachment between children and parents (or other caregivers), as well as the damage that results from insufficient care and affection.[2, 3, 4, 5] To summarize their findings bluntly: institutionalized babies and toddlers often develop in abnormal ways. My brother Rick had spent his first two-plus years in the Colorado State Orphanage. His difficulties bonding with my parents, as well as his subsequent aggressions toward them, were predictable, perhaps even inevitable, given the emotional starkness he had experienced during his formative years of early childhood.

Our parents responded to Rick's problematic behaviors by arranging psychotherapy both for him and for the family. Several times each month, they drove Rick to sessions at Ft. Logan Mental Health Center in west Denver. Both Dan and I took part in other appointments. Whether or not these interventions helped in the short term, they didn't solve the long-term issues. Rick started lashing out physically against both parents. Assaults grew increasingly violent. This crescendo of attacks led to Rick's near-homicide of our father.

In the aftermath of that incident, the Ft. Logan psychiatrists told my parents, "Your family is the most difficult case of this sort we've ever seen"; and, given the severe risks likely if the status quo continued, they strongly recommended removing Rick from the family. My parents set up the family lawyer as a legal guardian; Rick went into a residential program at Ft. Logan for several months; and, on reaching age eighteen a few months later, he shifted to a halfway house near downtown Denver. He never returned to the family home. Within a year he moved to California to start a new life.[6]

The crisis had passed. In its aftermath, however, I felt disoriented, exhausted, and fearful. What if Rick came back and killed us all? Even if he never returned, what did his departure mean? I was relieved to see him leave, but I also felt on some level, a level that look me years to understand, that I'd witnessed a calamity most children imagine but few ever see take place. A sibling had screwed up so badly that *he was rejected from the family.* Was it possible that I might screw up, too? Screw up just as badly? Would my parents ever throw me out? Surely not! I was a Good Boy—cooperative, cheerful, congenial, well-behaved, and (in the public-school jargon already common in American culture) achievement-oriented. My parents would never evict such a nice kid. Yet I'm not surprised now, though it took me years to grasp what happened, that during my junior high years I shifted from being a good student to being an academic star. Except for gym class, where I participated without interest and performed without skill, I otherwise earned flawless grades, praise from teachers, and other accolades. At the annual "academic field day" that Merrill Junior High sponsored to underscore the importance of intellectual excellence, I won more first prize awards than anyone else in my seventh-grade class. Never mind that my parents regarded grades and prizes as unimportant, uninteresting, and irrelevant to true education. I was intent on proving to my parents by any means that I wasn't just a Good Boy, I was a Great Boy.

IV. Us vs. Them

Throughout my childhood and pre-teen years, I didn't like boys. My dislike had its deepest roots in my toxic relationship with Rick, but the nature of boyhood itself in 1950's America, too, made me wary toward my male peers. Most boys in our neighborhood—one of the many crackerbox suburbs that had sprung up around Denver following World War II—struck me as uninteresting, uncommunicative, baffling and abrasive. As the son of professors, I stood out as overly talkative, contemptibly studious, ignorant of popular culture, and focused on all the wrong things. I knew nothing about sports. I was indifferent to cars. I wasn't impressed by the era's pop musicians—Bobby Darren, Frankie Avalon, Ricky Nelson, Elvis. My fascination with science branded me peculiar. My delight in classical music and books earned mockery and derision. Most of the boys in my neighborhood saw me as, at best, an *egghead*. At worst I was a *pansy*—a label that baffled me, since neighbors grew those flowers in their gardens. Although I managed to get along with some boys, most of them bored me, left me uneasy, or frightened me.

Conversations often bogged down from the start.

Boy: "Who d'you think will win?"

Eddy: "Win what?"

[Incredulous stare.] "The *game!*"

"*What* game?"

[Amazed, contemptuous smile.] "The World Series, dodo brain."

"Oh."

"Don't you know *anything?*"

Worse yet, simply being in their presence create alarming, bewildering interactions.

Boy: "What're you staring at?"

Eddy: "Nothing."
"Must be *something.*"
"No, really—nothing."
"Sure *seems* like something."
"Honest, it's nothing."
"Must be a pretty big *nothing.*"
"Look, can't we just drop it?"
"You'd *better* drop it."
"I'm trying."
[Pause.] *"What did you say?"*
"I said *I'm trying to mind my own business*—if you'll give me a chance."

At this point I would become aware of intense, unpleasant scrutiny. The boy facing me would stare without any comprehensible expression on his face. What did that blank stare mean? Was he going to punch me? Probably not. Time after time, nothing happened. To my surprise and relief, I discovered throughout boyhood and adolescence that my small size reduced rather than increased the risk of getting roughed up or beaten. Most boys viewed me as simply not worth the trouble. Even so, I often felt close to the edge. Would I end up running home with a bloody nose? Most of the time I figured out a gambit for departure, then walked away, relieved but baffled by how this pointless exchange had sprouted out of nowhere and flourished like a poisonous weed.[7]

Under these circumstances it's not surprising that I grasped at around this time how much I liked girls. In fact, I liked them at lot. The common wisdom among preteen boys was that girls were icky, annoying, *stoopid.* They were boring, silly, prissy, too polite, and too eager to please adults. Worst of all, girls were *girlish.* Most boys held most girls in contempt. One of the most insulting things a boy could call another boy was *girly,* or (fighting words now) *a girl.* If you had a high voice or a silly laugh, you sounded *girlish.* If you couldn't run fast or with good form, you *ran like a girl.* If you couldn't pitch a ball right, you *threw like a girl.* The arts, especially poetry and classical music, were *girl stuff.* In short, girls were ridiculous. Anything girls liked—or whatever girls had been coaxed, cajoled, or pressured into liking—was therefore ridiculous. Little or nothing about girls warranted any attention from pre-adolescent boys growing up in the 1950's. I went along with these notions for a while, though not without perplexity and unease. My parents, whom I loved and respected, held literature, classical music, and all the arts in high regard. They supported and encouraged my interest in writing fiction and poetry. They paid no attention to sports, and they never criticized my own my own indifference. Most of the people we knew within the academic community held similar views. If they valued these supposedly girlish activities and interests, what did their approval say about girls? What in turn did that say about me? For these and other reasons, I started to wonder about girls as early as ages five or six and with great focus from age eight on. Girls began to be appealing. They seemed generally smarter, more verbal, funnier, less chaotic, and much less violent than boys. I liked the sense of order they brought to the classroom. I liked the way they solved conflicts among themselves without shoving or shouting. I liked how they could express affection in ways that didn't involve wrestling or punching. With most of them I could carry on interesting conversations on many topics. Boys talked mostly about sports—one of the few subjects that didn't interest me. With girls I could discuss pets, nature, books, music, science, and travel. Girls' verbal facility and animated conversations impressed me most of all. Girls appeared to be more aware of more different aspects of the world than boys were; they could speak about them in more detail; and they could describe, and were willing to describe, what they were thinking and feeling. Girls seemed vivid. Boys seemed pale and drab. I decided at some point that girls lived in color, while boys lived in black-and-white.

I felt continuously drawn to them. At times my enthusiasm got the best of me. Just a few months into first grade, I impulsively reached over to Debbie Nerone, a girl I found delightful, and I kissed her hand. This act scandalized our classmates, prompting giggles from the girls and insults from the boys, some of whose mocking comments flared up for months afterwards. (Bruce Crow admonished me darkly: *"Crime doesn't pay!"*) A year or two later, during a two-family picnic in the Rockies, I fell suddenly in love with a seven-year-old named Ellen Hall, the daughter of a famous anthropologist, and I felt stunned and thrilled when she returned my affection. Expressing our mutual delight and admiration consisted entirely of holding hands as we sat and talked beside a mountain lake several hundred yards away from our parents and our potentially derisive siblings. Just "puppy love"? Perhaps. Or perhaps a deeper, if primordial, experience of marveling at another human being's existence? In any case, my expressions of enthusiasm for girls, most often limited to words rather than kisses, were a six-year-old's equivalent of Miranda's famous gush in *The Tempest:* "O brave new world, that has such creatures in it."

Even so, I often found girls perplexing. In groups they often talked all at once in ways that left me dizzy. I couldn't understand their games and couldn't master the skills necessary to play. Jacks happened too fast for me to follow. Jump-rope clearly required superhuman agility and speed. Their playground rhymes and camp songs evaded my understanding and defied my efforts to mimic. Worse yet was my awareness that a given topic of conversation wasn't necessarily what they were discussing; some other layer, some other subject, lay under the surface beyond what I could detect and far beyond what I could understand. For these and other reasons girls were both appealing, often longed-for, yet beyond reach.

Into this backdrop my friendship with Steve Fedder emerged and developed. We had grown up in the same neighborhood— our houses were just three blocks apart—and we had attended the same elementary school starting in kindergarten. During some years we had the same homeroom teacher. I can't recall a time when we weren't friends; we often teamed up on classroom projects; we played together at recess; and over the years, especially from third or fourth grades on, we hung out at each other's homes. During the summer months we became more or less inseparable. We rode around the neighborhood on our bikes. We undertook projects in our yards, often in mine, which was the largest in the neighborhood. These projects included constructing forts of various kinds, digging deep holes in our garden, and assembling kits typical of the era—models, transistor radios, and, later on, rockets.[8] We also watched TV together, usually at Steve's house. Typical of children and teens trying to figure out the world, we spent long hours together just talking about other people—our parents, Steve's sister and my brothers, kids at school, teachers, astronauts, and a small number of politicians (John Kennedy was a frequent topic). Unlike almost all the other boys I knew, Steve could speak openly, thoughtfully, and insightfully on many subjects. Each of us found that nothing was off limits. We could describe not only what we thought but what we felt without fear of criticism or mockery.

Among other things, this shared openness led to discussing the significant differences between our two families. Steve's parents, transplants from Chicago to Denver, were both evangelical Christians. His mother, Freda, a devout Lutheran, was rigorous in her expectations that Steve and his sister, Ginny, adhere to the Way, the Truth, and the Life. His father, Earl, was less devout than Freda despite being the son of a Lutheran pastor. My own parents were academic bohemians—my father a leftist professor of philosophy, raised Presbyterian but now agnostic and skeptical, to say the least, of organized religion; my mother, a lapsed Mexican-American Catholic capable of greater charity toward other people and more innate spirituality than most churchgoers I've ever met. Theologically, the Fedders and the Myerses couldn't have been much different. Church attendance was a topic that the two sets of parents simply avoided. For these and other ideological reasons, I felt surprised (once I grasped the issues) that Freda and Earl so readily allowed their son to maintain such a close friendship with a freethinking, "unchurched" boy.

My own family, meanwhile, provided a setting that offered both nurturance and complex challenges. Despite my almost constant conflicts with my brother Rick, the household felt positive overall. Both of my parents taught at the University of Denver—my father in the philosophy department, my mother in the department of modern languages. Both were intelligent, kind, and loving. They had a wide circle of friends in the academic community. Our 1900-era farmhouse served as a meeting place for scholars, writers, and artists. Among those present was Irwin Goodenough, a historian of religion and a scholar of Hellenistic influences on Judaism. An occasional visitor was Cham Hendon, a painter whose figurative work received wide recognition later on, during the 1970's and 80's. Sir Karl Popper, one of the leading figures in 20th-century philosophy of science, once came for dinner. Present on many occasions was John Williams, a well-regarded novelist (who, a decade later, won the National Book Award for his novel *Augustus*). Once or twice my family hosted S.I. Hayakawa, linguist, semanticist, and future U.S. senator. With these intellectuals and artists cycling through the household, I grew up excited about intellectual inquiry and artistic endeavor. My parents valued thinking, talking, speculating, and creating. These weren't just valued activities, however; they were viewed as *normal* activities. Even by the age of twelve I, too, fancied myself an intellectual and an artist. I sometimes felt challenged, however, even stressed, as I tried to keep up with the discussions. I also felt confused as I started perceiving contradictions among these *cognoscenti* and *literati,* including the realization that people with brilliant minds could have unpleasant, even loathsome, personalities. One professor in the philosophy department, for instance—a European-born, quadrilingual polymath who, among other things, had studied physics under Albert Einstein during the 1930's and had served in the OSS during World War II—was a brilliant scholar but a manipulative, narcissistic, abusive man. I watched in fear and disgust one afternoon when he made an aggressive pass at a colleague's wife right there in our living room: called her a whore to her face and swatted her buttocks. Weren't professors supposed to be thoughtful, ethical, and committed to bringing forth the Light of Reason? I couldn't make sense of what sometimes appeared to be these men's self-serving, preening statements. Some professors' occasional aggressive or salacious behavior toward women, especially, confused and demoralized me. In addition, the sheer intensity of academics' and artists' conversations—the ebb and flow of ideas, the riptides of wit, the tsunamis of disquisition—left me exhausted. How great a relief, then, to escape from these accomplished but self-impressed adults and find more easy-going companionship with a smart friend my own age.

What developed between Steve and me was a friendship of a type that probably occurs most often in childhood and adolescence: a friendship that is both self-contained, even insular, but that simultaneously allows and encourages exploration of the world. We could collaborate in trying to make sense of the mysteries, marvels, contradictions, and stupidities we perceived all around us as we grew up together. I suspect that this sense of alliance and comradeship—Us vs. Them— is common among both boys and girls during childhood and the teen years. The nature of boys' friendships, however, isn't well understood. The social science literature on this topic tends to summarize girls' friendships as being more deeply connected than boys' equivalents. For instance, Deborah Tannen's 1990 bestseller *You Just Don't Understand: Women and Men in Conversation*, popularized a notion that girls value intimacy and connection with others, while boys value "pack behavior" and have emotionally shallow relationships. This widely accepted view implies that boys don't need close bonds with other boys.[9] Tannen's perception of "boy culture" seems uncomfortably familiar to me from my own experiences during the 1950's and 60's. At the same time, I longed for deeper communication with other people, boys and girls alike. My frustrations with other boys resulted chiefly from finding them less verbal and less articulate than the companions I wanted. I lived in this sense on both sides of the fence: as a boy who found most boys exasperating, yet simultaneously as a boy who found companionship and intellectual stimulation among a few smart, supportive male peers.[10]

In any case, I could raise issues with Steve that I wouldn't even mention with other friends, or would do so at great risk. We discussed what we liked and disliked about our parents. We criticized Steve's sister and my brothers. For the first time in our lives, we talked politics—his parents' conservatism, my parents' liberalism—with each family's beliefs providing a revelation to the other. We argued about religion—the existence (or not) of God; the veracity (if any) of the Bible; the purpose (or pointlessness) of institutional churches. We explored our hopes and fears for the future—college, careers, marriage, parenthood. In an era when most boys learned about sex chiefly from *Playboy* and from peers' locker-room boasts, Steve and I found my parents' copy of *Ideal Marriage: Its Physiology and Technique,* a 1920's-vintage sex manual, read it together, and speculated about the mysteries of female anatomy, physiology, and psychology that the book unveiled.[11] (The author, a Dutch gynecologist named Theodoor Hendrik van de Velde, wrote this and other books to counteract the sexual ignorance resulting from Victorian and post-Victorian prudery. Although derided as salacious in its own era and mocked as risible during the 1960's sexual revolution, *Ideal Marriage* became the bestselling sex manual of all time, reprinted forty-six times in its original edition.) Steve and I discovered at some point that the dust jacket for a music reference guide I owned, *The Beethoven*

Encyclopedia, precisely fit *Ideal Marriage,* so we handily cloaked the manual in the music book's guise, so much the better to shelve it in my own bedroom for easy access. If my mom or dad inquired, "What are you boys up to?" I would answer—always aware of my parents' enthusiasm for my interest in classical music—"Nothing much, just looking up stuff in *The Beethoven Encyclopedia.*"

What Steve and I attained over the years, what we collaborated to create, was an alliance of two boys in a baffling, sometimes threatening era. I suspect that Steve didn't find the world as daunting as I did. He was bigger, more handsome, and more confident than I. He moved easily among different social groups at school. My origins in an academic family prompted me to feel guarded and arrogant in ways that created far more obstacles than what other people put in my path. The truth remained: both of us felt what all teenagers feel, a perplexity about and fascination with almost everything around us. All the better, then, that each of us allied himself with the other, teamed up to figure out the strange world, found solace in shared interests, and offered mutual support.

And, in a figurative and literal crescendo over the years, we could build lots of fireworks, rockets, and bombs.

V. The Cookbook and the Kitchen

For years, both Steve and I had done what most boys did in the weeks leading up to July Fourth: we bought fireworks and set them off. These were the sacraments in American boys' holy vernal rites. Steve and I, either with our families present or on our own, ignited these devices and enjoyed the spectacles they created. Inverted cones of sparks spewed into the air. Colored balls of fire flew off like startled birds. Odd little aluminum whirligigs spun away, buzzing. Skinny rockets trailed sparks as they shot upward and vanished with a bang. Firecrackers boomed one by one or in a stuttering cacophony of explosions. For us and for most kids in our neighborhood, setting off these fireworks was an almost nightly pastime starting many days or even weeks before the Fourth and reaching its gaudiest, loudest, smelliest, most chaotic conclusion on the big night itself.

It's not surprising that as the years passed, however, commercially available fireworks started to seem tedious. What delights an eight- or nine-year-old boy or girl can easily bore a pre-teen or a teenager. The colored flames no longer dazzled; the sparks ceased to delight; the bangs lost their ability to startle. By age eleven or twelve, Steve and I grew restless. We grew *critical*. Mass-produced Asian products started to look gimmicky and flimsy. Their cost, too, began to seem greater than the pleasure they provided. We wanted literally more bang for the buck. Was it possible, Steve and I wondered, that we could do better? Could we make more impressive fireworks ourselves than what we could buy? Best of all, could we produce what we coveted during more than just a few weeks each summer? We decided to explore the options. Dissecting fountains and Roman candles revealed what lay inside the paper tubes. Splitting open Black Cats showed us how just a little powder created a big explosion. Dismantling these devices led quickly to a further insight: we could combine the contents of two or more small fireworks and make something more powerful. Rolling and gluing a tube from newsprint, capping one end of the tube with a wooden plug, filling the tube with powder from several ordinary fountains, and capping the other end with a second plug—this end now perforated with a single aperture—could create a mega-fountain. Emptying the powder from a dozen Black Cats and packing the accumulation into a cardboard casing easily produced a flashier, louder explosive.

At some point Steve spotted an enticing advertisement in the back pages of either *Popular Mechanics* or *Mechanix Illustrated*. There, among ads boasting EARN BIG MONEY and LEARN TV REPAIR AT HOME and BE RUGGED! COMMAND

RESPECT! he spotted the headline PYROTECHNIC COOK-BOOK. The brief text read something like: "Make your own fountains, pinwheels, skyrockets, and firecrackers." The ad specified a modest price and provided a mailing address. Steve sent away and soon received a crudely printed, hand-stapled booklet. Suddenly we had lists of ingredients and step-by-step instructions for creating the fireworks we coveted. Best of all, the cookbook specified sources for obtaining pyrotechnic chemicals. From that moment onward, new vistas opened.

It's unclear to me why Steve's mother and father allowed us to set up a fireworks factory in their family's garage. Overall, Earl and Freda were strict parents. Neither do I understand why even my more permissive mom and dad let me experiment with flammable, explosive, often toxic chemicals. Steve and I didn't proceed in secret; we explained to both sets of parents what we were doing. Freda and Earl, entering their own garage, could easily see the equipment that their son and his friend had acquired, along with the tidy little drum-like containers of ingredients that Steve and I sent away for, received in the mail, and arrayed on a shelf along with Earl's bottles of lawn poison and packets of rose fertilizer. Were Freda and Earl, or were my own parents, concerned about what two teenage boys might concoct in this rudimentary lab? When I asked Steve this question recently, he answered: "I'm surprised they didn't object. I guess they just trusted us. They probably felt that we'd be careful. Freda even drove me across town at one point to a company that sold concentrated nitric acid and iodine crystals. She had to sign for me, since these chemicals weren't available for sale to minors." My own parents likewise trusted what I was doing. In an age when commercially available chemistry sets for kids contained many substances that would now be prohibited even for use in high school or college classes, the notion of two intelligent, well-behaved boys concocting flammable, explosive compounds without supervision somehow wasn't outside the normal limits.[12]

We soon organized and instituted an R&D project to design and construct fireworks. Less than a laboratory, the workshop for these efforts resembled a rudimentary kitchen—a small space stocked with measuring cups, spoons, mixing bowls, and a mortar and pestle. The cookbook now in our possession contained recipes no more complex than what we might have found in *The Joy of Cooking* if Steve and I had decided to bake blueberry muffins. We had no other instruction manual; we needed nothing else. We simply brainstormed the items we wanted to create. (Using a pseudo-Teutonic accent that we fancied a secret language, we called our inventions *krahks* and *voorks*.) Steve, whose grasp of chemistry at age twelve or thirteen exceeded mine even now, over five decades later, would figure out which ingredients we needed and how to combine them. The cookbook provided the basic instructions; Steve's insights guided us further. Soon our ideas and the concepts we mastered began to flower into brilliant, loud reality.

Our experiments dazzled us in ways that went well beyond the fireworks' gaudy effects. The attributes of different chemicals drew our attention, fascination, and admiration. Creating colors was just one instance of how *specific* these chemicals could be. Strontium nitrate and other strontium salts produced red fire. To create orange, we used calcium carbonate or calcium chloride. Yellow? That required sodium nitrate or sodium oxalate. For green, we used barium salts like barium nitrate. Purple: a combination of copper and strontium compounds. Blue? Copper acetoarsenite ("Paris green"—a highly toxic compound used as a rodenticide and insecticide). Red: strontium nitrate. Magnesium and aluminum generated intense silver light. To create sparks, we stirred iron filings into the mixture. Other effects required other compounds. To create a crackling noise, granules of bismuth trioxide or bismuth subcarbonate would combust rapidly, causing the crackle effect. Whistling fireworks required gallic acid, sodium salicylate, or potassium benzoate. Best of all, at least in the minds of two teenage boys, was the chemistry of explosions. Lampblack (finely ground charcoal) mixed with sulfur flour and saltpeter (potassium nitrate) created a simple, reliable, potent blackpowder. The fact that these chemicals combined to induce effects so different from their component parts: this impressed us. Removing even one of the substances immediately rendered the other two ineffective. Charcoal mixed with sulfur: almost inert. Charcoal and saltpeter: not much better. Sulfur and saltpeter: likewise. Combine all three, however, and we unleashed great power.

I felt constantly amazed that a limited number of chemicals—fewer than two dozen, for our purposes—could combine to create such an outrageous variety of phenomena. A mere one hundred eighteen elements created all phenomena in the universe. Most remarkable was that these phenomena were *orderly.* If Steve and I followed the recipes, we could predict the consequences. Matter behaved in organized ways. There was no magic here, although the effects we produced could be powerful, sometimes bizarre, often dazzling to the eye and stunning to the ear. Yet the consistency and the *precision* of matter ultimately impressed me even more than the flash-bang razzle-dazzle of the fireworks. (And Steve as well. In high school, he showed abundant talent in the humanities but focused on studies of the physical sciences; then he majored in chemistry during his undergraduate years, obtained a Ph.D. in chemistry during graduate school, and went on to a distinguished, decades-long career of teaching chemistry at a well-regarded private university.)

Our kitchen now fully stocked, Steve and I went to work cooking our recipes. Early efforts focused on fountains. We had delighted for many years in the brilliant eruptions that even commercial products created: geysers of flames, colors, and sparks. Now regarding the store-bought fountains as weak and short-lived, however, we invented far better variants. Rolling our own cylindrical cases, packing them with a greater quantity of powder, and installing a reliable aperture by gluing a perforated penny to the underside of the upper wooden plug, Steve and I created fountains that burned longer, faster, louder, and more brilliantly than any we had ever seen before. Commercial fountains spewed sparks only four to six feet into the air; ours shot a column of fire and sparks eight, ten, twelve feet high. The spectacle lasted two or three times as long as the ordinary products. Everyone we allowed to see them in action—our parents, our siblings, and a select group of friends and neighbors—oohed and ahhed and proclaimed these the best fountains ever.

This victory soon inspired a related project: pinwheels. Here again we regarded the commercial version of these products as limited, even pathetic. Our own pinwheels were bigger and much more powerful. Rather than mounting puny tubes on cardboard wheels, Steve and I cut hexagons out of scrap lumber, then attached homemade fountains on three of the flat edges, left the intervening three edges empty, and connected the fountains with lengths of wick to create serial ignition. Once more our creations were more powerful and delightful than the ordinary products that we now held in contempt.

Other inventions? Cascades, little packets of powder and color-producing chemicals, which hung from a string and dropped waterfalls of light and sparks onto the ground. Homemade rockets, complete with nosecones and fins—far more impressive than the anorectic bottle rockets that most kids found so amusing. We called these pocket rockets—sometimes *pookit rookits*—because of their compact size and shape. We also found it amusing that we could concoct powerful rocket fuel from finely ground saltpeter combined with, of all things, confectioners' sugar. (How sweet that a crucial component for making flammable propellant was the same ingredient our mothers used to ice cakes.)

Best of all, perhaps, were the rapid advancements we made in devising our own explosives. We knew that local boys, including some we regarded as obnoxious and hostile, viewed themselves as tough because of their access to firecrackers. Black Cats? Kids' stuff! Some of these boys set off cherry bombs and even M-80's, notorious for creating the loudest, most startling booms on summer nights. Steve and I could do far better. Previously limited to the substances we could extract from commercial firecrackers, we now made our own explosive powders. We mixed it in large quantities. We produced it so well and so abundantly that in the local arms race among the neighbor-boys, Steve and I felt that we ruled the world.

VI. Liftoff

At some point during the early 1960's, when I was eleven or twelve, I noticed an advertisement at the back of an issue of *Boys' Life*. The ad was for Estes Industries, a company that produced and sold model rockets. I sent away for an Estes catalogue and received it a week or two later in the mail. Then I read words that poured gasoline—or rocket fuel—on the flames of my curiosity and imagination.

> Imagine the thrill of pressing the firing switch and watching a rocket you have built roar skyward in a cloud of smoke, leaving a vapor trail behind as it shrinks into just a speck. Then at the apex of its flight, a streamer or parachute blossoms out, returning the rocket to the earth undamaged, ready for another flight.

At that point in my life, I couldn't imagine a much more exciting sight.

> But there is more to model rocketry than this. Not only is it thrilling, but it provides an unexcelled opportunity to study and learn space science, to begin studying for a career dedicated to pushing man's

frontiers farther and farther towards the stars. Scores of young rocketeers today are finding the value of model rocketry in science fair projects, school projects, and in their own private research programs.[13]

Rockets had fascinated me for many years. During the late 1950's I had followed NASA's early, often unsuccessful launches. More effective U.S. efforts during the 1960's impressed and delighted me: Alan Shepherd's suborbital flight in 1961, John Glenn's orbital mission in early 1962, and the Gemini orbits that followed. I eagerly awaited the Apollo program's moon landings, scheduled to start in the late 1960's. During those early years of the space race I played with toy rockets and started experimenting with powered models. One of my favorite Christmas presents was an Alpha II, a well-designed, well-made plastic rocket—ten inches tall and powered by fuel made from vinegar and baking soda—which I received at age ten. The solid-fuel rockets that became available a few years later extended my longstanding interest and offered a tangible, complex, powerful reality after years of dreaming.

My early projects went by the book. Estes model rockets, made of paper tubes, balsa fins and nose cones, and other light materials, held at that time, and continue to maintain, an almost flawless safety record. I powered the kits with the single-use solid-fuel engines that Estes Industries had carefully engineered and mass-produced. Although I was the chief instigator, Steve soon collaborated with me in these projects. We launched our rockets in fields and schoolyards using the Estes electrical ignition gadget and ten or fifteen feet of wiring that kept us at a safe distance. My dad supervised. These rocketry projects were, in short, part of a mainstream, above-board hobby. Yet even these lightweight models conferred a great sense of power. Compared to Fourth of July bottle rockets, they were bigger, faster, more sophisticated, and much more impressive. Several Estes kits were modeled after NASA rockets of the early Space Race: the Atlas, the Redstone, and the massive Saturn V. Others resembled U.S. missiles of the Cold War era: the Bomarc, the Minuteman, and the Jupiter. Model rocketry may have been a hobby, but for Steve and me it also became a doorway into the realm of aerospace technology— the design issues, the underlying math, the laws of physics, the process of R&D.

Our experiments soon branched out from the mail-order kits that we had begun to find routine and unimaginative. Instead of following the instructions, we cooked up our own designs. We built rockets, for instance, that took the basic principle of staging to absurd heights, literally: models with four, five, six, or more boosters—two was the recommended maximum—that reached altitudes of two or three thousand feet. (Most of those multi-stage rockets shot upward and disappeared forever.) I also designed two different kinds of hand-held launchers— essentially bazookas—one of which featured a Victrola horn-like bell and resembled a mega-blunderbuss out of a science fiction movie. Perhaps most imaginative was a flying saucer, fifteen inches in diameter and fashioned from a polished, painted Styrofoam disk, whose laterally mounted rocket motors rotated the disc at hundreds of RPMs. Thirty angled fins around the periphery created sufficient lift to launch the saucer upwards. The riskiest project, however, was a category of rocket that contained an M-80 firecracker in its payload compartment. When I designed this system, I specified an electrical contact switch to serve as a detonator, setting up the rocket to explode on impact. In short, this missile contained a warhead. Steve and I grasped even at the time that we had created a miniature ICBM—one that we somehow had the sense not to build.

Does this pint-sized R&D program mean that we were pre-cocious aerospace engineers? Or does it mean that aerospace engineers are superannuated junior-high schoolboys? All I know is that while attending junior high, I was mimicking and in some sense acting out the U.S.-Soviet missile race. I and perhaps most youthful rocketeers were doing obeisance to the Cold War weapons supposedly keeping us safe from the Soviets. Even the Estes approach to rocketry—professionally designed, lightweight models powered by industrially manufactured engines—sanctioned the connection between a boyish pastime and the looming geopolitical issues. The company's 1963 catalogue gave an explicit imprimatur to this hobby: "The type of youth[ful] science study provided by model rocketry is necessary if this country is to survive the coming years of the Cold War and, if it should ever arise, a major war." Even a kid building paper-and-balsa models in his bedroom could be a soldier in America's battle against the USSR.

VII. The Position

During the 1950's and '60's, the Cold War tainted every aspect of American culture. The U.S.-Soviet rivalry and the tensions it spawned were evident in the news and in government pronouncements but also everywhere in American material culture, entertainment, and politics. Movies of the era provide only the most glaring examples: not just *On the Beach* and *Dr. Strangelove* but the scores of sci-fi movies—*Godzilla, The Day the World Ended, It Came from beneath the Sea,* and *Them!*—in which mutant creatures personify the nuclear age and the dread its dangers spread throughout the world. In addition, the iconography of the Cold War appeared almost everywhere. In *Duck and Cover,* a novel I wrote for children many decades later, the opening paragraph conjures a kid's-eye view of how the era's nuclear imagery suffused everything:

> That spring, when Andy MacLane was eleven, the whole world seemed to be turning into missiles. Play Land, the local toy store, filled its front window with toy missiles—rockets, bombs, and spaceships. The housewares department at Sears displayed a toaster shaped like a squat little missile. Woolworth's sold

a flashlight that resembled a silvery missile. There was a restaurant in town called the Atomic Diner that pointed skyward from the ground like a huge missile's metal nose cone. At Elitch's, the local amusement park, Andy rode on some missile-shaped rdes: the H-bomb, the Rocket, and the Nuke. And the cars he saw—Chevies, Buicks, Chryslers, Fords, and especially Cadillacs—all had fins as big and pointy as the ones on the missiles in a Buck Rogers sci-fi movie. No matter where he looked, Andy saw missiles.

The year was 1962 . . .

Steve and I were both born in 1950. Five years earlier, in mid-July of 1945, the United States had detonated the first atomic bomb at Alamogordo, then had dropped Little Boy on Hiroshima and Fat Man on Nagasaki a few weeks later. In 1949, the Soviet Union had exploded its own A-bomb. The Cold War had bloomed into a tenacious, toxic flower by the time we entered kindergarten. Steve and I, along with all other members of the Boomer generation, grew up participating in routine Duck and Cover drills at school. I can't recall any time after age seven when I wasn't aware of nuclear war as a constant possibility. If I ever needed reminding, the frequent, unavoidable drills brought the situation back into my full awareness.

We would be right in the middle of a spelling test, a civics lesson, or an art project, when suddenly loud bells would start ringing in the hallway—three short rings, then a pause, then another three, repeated many times. All of the kids understood the message: *Duck and cover!* Most of us would immediately crouch under our desks and assume The Position: kneeling, hunching low, and placing one arm across the back of the head and the other across the eyes. A few kids, mostly boys, would just sit there, staring at our teacher, Mrs. Johnson. "You heard the bells!" she would shout in amazement and exasperation.

"Duck and cover!" Then even the stragglers would crawl beneath their desks and assume The Position.

I would already be on the floor crouching obediently—cowering—not at all convinced that this was a drill. Waves of sadness and fear would wash through me. I couldn't believe I'd die so young. Eleven years old! I'd never have a chance to grow up. I'd never learn to drive or go to college. I'd never leave Denver and go off to explore the world. I'd never become a brilliant scientist. I'd never win the Nobel Prize and return from Sweden after the ceremony to find myself famous throughout America. The cruelty and unfairness of the situation brought tears to my eyes and a sour taste to my throat.

Huddling under my desk, I would wait in The Position. Five minutes would pass. Ten. Fifteen. All of the kids grew restless, some muttering and groaning, a few even calling out with requests or complaints: "Mrs. Johnson, can I go to the bathroom?" or "When's the all-clear?" or "Get your elbow *out of my face!"* The Position grew increasingly uncomfortable as the drill went on, but I was always too scared to move or talk or do anything but wait. Every drill felt like the longest ever. At some point I would tell myself: *This can't be a drill. This is the real thing.* The teachers were just trying to keep us calm by *telling* us it was a drill. Russian missiles were heading over the North Pole and streaking toward John J. Cory Elementary School in Denver, Colorado, even as we cowered in our classroom trying to keep still and maintain The Position.

Then at long last the all-clear bell would ring. We would all get off the floor, stretch, and sit at our desks again. Sometimes we would emerge to find Mr. Wilkins, the gym teacher, standing up front with Mrs. Johnson. Mr. Wilkins, one of only two male teachers at Cory School, was in charge of the drills. His supervisory role probably derived from that era's assumption that a man would be the best captain at the helm during such a serious, even life-threatening crisis; or it may have been based on his military background. (We students never knew exactly what Mr. Wilkins had done during the war, but he referred to hearing loss resulting from gunfire and explosions.) In addition, the principal and other teachers may have assumed, rightly, that no students would argue with or disobey Mr. Wilkins. This assumption was accurate not because he was harsh or even stern, but because all the kids loved him—the boys because he was big and strong and knowledgeable about sports; the girls because he was so handsome and polite. These last two aspects of his nature won Mr. Wilkins many admirers. More than once I heard girls and women comparing him to Paul Newman. I had no idea who Paul Newman was and didn't care. The reality was that even I liked Mr. Wilkins. Despite his being the male gym teacher and clearly athletic and strong, he never made fun of me for being bad at sports, a dispensation that no other coach granted during my entire school career; and besides, Mr. Wilkins also taught the fifth- and sixth-grade science classes, which I loved. In any case, Mr. Wilkins now delivered The Duck and Cover Speech. "Ladies and gentlemen, I don't believe you understand the seriousness of what we're doing," Mr. Wilkins would tell us as we settled into our seats. "No, I don't see any signs of that. Mr. Brink, do you think I'm doing this for my health? Mr. Lysaght? Mr. Crow? What would have happened if this hadn't been a drill? What would have happened if a Soviet missile had detonated at just that moment over downtown Denver? Hmm? Tell me that."

The speech would go on for what seemed a long time. Mr. Wilkins never showed any anger, just a mix of disappointment, sadness, amazement, and some kind of mild contempt. Then he would thank Mrs. Johnson and leave.

I would feel deep relief and a strange kind of delight, of course, that this drill had been only a drill. Once again we had performed the bizarre Duck and Cover ritual. Once again we had survived. Yet once again I came away with the realization that muddling through a drill didn't guarantee that the next one wouldn't be The Real Thing. Unlike most of the kids I knew at the time, I read the newspapers. I followed the confusing, alarming progress of the Cold War. I knew that Colorado, though far from Washington, D.C., was high on the Soviets' list of nuclear targets because of the NORAD facility south of Denver and the numerous federal facilities just a few miles west of where I lived. I knew that if Soviet missiles struck my city, all of us there would die within a few minutes.

My response? Deep dread, low-grade anxiety, and a sickening belief that my life would soon be over. To express my fears, I wrote stories featuring rockets, bombs, and mushroom clouds; I drew pictures of missiles streaking across the sky and of cities erupting into firestorms; I built plastic models of fighter jets, bombers, and ICBMs; I lined them up on my shelves like offerings in a shrine for a god I hoped to propitiate. It's no coincidence that my interest in model rocketry started around 1961, the year of the Berlin Blockade Crisis and its near-triggering of a U.S.-Soviet shooting war, and that my interest intensified into an obsession during 1962, the year of the Cuban Missile Crisis. During the Cuban emergency that October, I was convinced for an entire week that every day would be my last. Fellow students in our junior high found my dread annoying and my weepiness contemptible. Our teachers worked hard to reassure us that the crisis would inevitably resolve. Somehow the conflict didn't "go nuclear." Historians, however, now regard that week in October of 1962 as a hair's-breadth escape from Armageddon. (Arthur M. Schlesinger, Jr., an advisor to President Kennedy at the time and a historian of the era, has written that "This was not only the most dangerous moment of the Cold War. It was the most dangerous moment in human history.") In addition to aspects of the confrontation that were widely reported at the time—the U.S. naval blockade of Cuba, the downing of an American U-2 spy plane on October 27th, and a week of tense sessions at the U.N. General Assembly—several close calls occurred beyond public awareness throughout the crisis. Cuba's President, Fidel Castro, almost decided to take military action on this own. General Curtis LeMay, the hawkish Chief of Staff for the U.S. Air Force, attempted to pressure President Kennedy into bombing the Cuban missile sites pre-emptively. Most dangerous of all was the decision by Soviet submarine captains on patrol in the Caribbean to launch nuclear-armed torpedoes against American ships enforcing the naval blockade. On October 27th, only a countermanding order by Kapitan Vasili Arkhipov, head of the submarine fleet, prevented his fellow captains from taking this step. None of these developments reached public awareness until years or decades later. Even as a twelve year old, however, I somehow intuited during the crisis itself how close the world came to nuclear calamity. [14]

One might assume, then, that given all the missile imagery, the omnipresence of nuclear weapons in the news, the nearly universal worries about World War III, the genuine possibility of U.S.-Soviet warfare, and the near-catastrophe in 1962, that a sensitive, artistically inclined boy would have avoided and rejected everything to do with rockets and their warheads. That's not how the mind works. Mimicking and externalizing fears can be a way to manage them—even fears of injury, destruction, and death. Just as American boys played G.I.'s-versus-Krauts during World War II, so too did Iraqi boys play *jihadis*-versus-crusaders during the 2003 U.S. invasion and its chaotic aftermath, and so too have other boys imitated other conflicts. For these reasons and other reasons, it's clear to me now that on some level, Steve and I were acting out the Cold War not only in our nightmares but in our daytime hobbies. I can't speak for Steve, but I, at least, vented my anxiety and dread by replicating in miniature what loomed all around us. Small wonder that we ramped up our own private missile race, our own private Manhattan Project. [15]

VIII. Fearing, Geeking, Preening

But if we were acting out the Cold War, why? Were Steve and I just venting our anxieties about the prospect of nuclear annihilation? Or were we perhaps expressing more specific, local, personal anxieties as well, or instead? Here again I can't speak for Steve. He and I have discussed the issues in recent years, and neither of us has reached definitive conclusions about the psychological substrata underlying our pyrotechnic projects. We agree, however, that each of us must have been pushing back on some level against trauma we had experienced within our respective families. My trauma stemmed from years of my older brother's psychological abuse and, paradoxically, from the experience of seeing the abuser ejected from the family. I also felt less intense but chronic anxiety as I conflicted with boys in the neighborhood and at school. The results were built-up resentment, sadness, fear, and anger that erupted not only in metaphorical, psychological flames and explosions but, by means of pyrotechnic chemistry, in the real thing. Steve's situation was different but intense in its own way. "For me," he explained recently, "the trauma was associated with all the family's church stuff and my fear that I was going to go to hell." Earl and Freda Fedder were attentive, loving parents, but their evangelical precepts left Steve deeply anxious from early boyhood through his college years. Was it surprising that he might express some of these anxieties by concocting the earthly equivalents of fire and brimstone?

I see another issue energizing our pyrotechnic experiments. I was small for my age at every stage of boyhood. I was a skinny pre-teen before pubescence and remained a short, underweight teenager even once the testosterone tsunami swept through my body starting at age twelve. Although wiry and physically active—I had always been an excellent hiker, and in my late teens and twenties I became a skilled mountaineer—I had no interest or competence in playing team sports. My academic family's background, my intellectual talents, my studiousness, and my deep love of the arts prompted many of my peers, especially other boys, to label me an artsy-fartsy pansy egghead. These attributes, along with the arrogance and class snobbery they inspired in me, left me feeling isolated, defensive, resentful, and inclined toward counter-mockery. Fireworks and explosives became one of the several ways I told my peers *Fuck you*. Or, more accurately, told my male peers. The girls? They presented a different audience, one I addressed with a different message, a message spoken in a vocabulary of flames, whooshes, and booms that I hoped girls would find intriguing and impressive.

"Here's how rockets work," I told my fellow students when I made a presentation to our science class. I was twelve years old. Until that moment I had felt too shy to stand before my peers and say more than a few words; now I found myself expounding at length. I explained Isaac Newton's Third Law of Motion: how every action has an equal and opposite reaction. I noted that in accordance with this law, rockets didn't need anything to "push against." Gases ejected backward from a nozzle will move the rocket forward as a result of that equal, opposite reaction. I diagrammed a solid-fuel engine, named its parts, and explained their sequential functions. I displayed a variety of home-made rockets and noted their features. My classmates' reactions? Mixed. Some of the boys paid attention, others showed signs of impatience or indifference, and some looked contemptuous. But the girls: most seemed to be interested, even fascinated. Later, a few of them complimented me on my report. It's not that my female classmates necessarily shared my interest in the topic; the early Sixties were still an era when rocketry was a "boy's hobby." I sensed, however, that my knowledge and skill prompted the girls to take notice. This sense of the situation, whether accurate or not, delighted me. Generally speaking, the girls were better students than the boys. They were more attentive, more curious, more imaginative. I believed that my own intellectual and technical achievements could impress female peers whose respect I craved even as a pre-teen boy. In short, I believed that someone like me—someone in a category of people that American culture would soon start labeling nerds and geeks—could be perceived as interesting and even attractive. My intellectual and technical pursuits were, among other things, a kind of sexual preening.

Did the girls really care? Probably not. Only a few years later I began to realize that girls' and women's reactions to male preening consist mostly of amusement, derision, and strained patience. But teenage boys preen anyway, and strutting my pyrotechnic stuff was just my variant of what's probably a hardwired aspect of male behavior. Even so, I enjoyed putting on fireworks displays for girls I knew and, during my later teens, for my girlfriends. My first sweetheart, Mindy, clearly enjoyed the spectacle of homemade fountains. A later girlfriend, Anita, was perhaps less impressed but willing to admit that the sparks, flames, and colors were visually beautiful. As George Plimpton notes in his book on the subject, "[F]ireworks provided a sort of equalizer, especially for those kids who were not good at sports."[16]

Was there another sexual aspect to these projects? Maybe so. It's not difficult to grasp the symbolism of this outpouring from an adolescent boy's unconscious. At that age I felt as if my blood were 100% testosterone. My body, boiling with desire, resonated to the presence of the womanly girls around me, yet I had no outlet beyond self-administering the sexual first-aid universal among teenage boys. Were fireworks a symbolic expression of pent-up sexual energy? To perceive a tube gushing a spray of sparks and fire as analogous to adolescent male eruptions is risible, of course, if not contemptible. Yet in the mind itself this imagery is neither far-fetched nor solely a male fantasy. Years later, one of my girlfriends spoke of her own orgasms in these terms: "When I come, my body explodes with light." Equally far-fetched? Not really. Some people I've spoken with, including women, describe perceiving brilliant lights and colors during sexual relations. Recent studies using fMRI technology to scan both men and women at the point of climax show the brain literally alight with electrical activity. It's interesting, too, that a common nickname for intense lovemaking is "fireworks." When I researched aspects of this essay through Google, the search terms "books about fireworks" brought up far more romance novels than pyrotechnic manuals. It's not surprising that an adolescent boy, deprived of sex with the girls I longed for, might vent some of his libido through fireworks; might, indeed, create some spectacular eruptions; and might, as I joked even at the time, "Get my rockets off."

IX. Mastery and Control

Now, over fifty years after Steve and I concluded our pyrotechnic R&D program, I continue to wonder what purpose it served. Were we just preening? Displaying our bright peacock tails—made not of feathers but of flames and sparks—before the neighbor kids? Attempting to impress the girls? Sounding our *barbaric yawp over the rooftops of the world,* in Whitman's phrase? Shouting *Fuck you!* at the World War II generation, which often seemed unreliable, dangerous, and, indeed, willing to blow up the entire human species? Did I somehow exorcize the Cold War demon from my soul? Did I expunge the anger I felt toward my brother Rick for his many years of abuse? Did I ease the anxiety I experienced following his forced exile from the family? Did I simply vent testosterone-charged adolescent energy? Maybe some, all, or none of the above. I believe that beyond just preening, shouting, and venting, however, I was exploring ways to gain mastery over life. Oliver Sacks comments thoughtfully on his own similar experience: "The special dangers of chemistry were sought out, to some degree," he writes, ". . . as a means of playing with such fears, persuading myself that by care and vigilance, prudence, forethought, one could learn to control, or find a way through, this hazardous world." Steve and I, each of us in his own way, were doing our equivalents. For me, the hazards included not just the rigidities and aggressions of 1950's and 60's boy culture but also, and especially, the constant anxieties of the Cold War era and the ever-present risks of nuclear annihilation. Is it amusing, even contemptible, that my response included expressing my anxiety and anger through pyrotechnic chemistry? Some people will think so. Sacks remarks about himself, however, in ways that apply to me as well: "[T]hrough care and luck, I . . . could maintain a sense of mastery and control."[17] If nothing else, this statement is a terse summary of a primary task that all adolescents must undertake as they work their way toward adulthood.

Nor am I surprised that during this same time, my mind erupted into another kind of pyrotechnics. Under the tutelage of several teachers from seventh through twelfth grades, and with the guidance of my supportive parents, I started exploring how words, too, can combine like chemicals and foster trans-formations. Words can form potent compounds—metaphors, similes, turns of phrase—fully as powerful as lampblack, sulfur, and saltpeter erupting as blackpowder. I discovered that I could create fire, sparks, colors, and explosions on the page. With great focus and intensity, I started writing stories, poems, essays, and articles. The literary arts became an obsession, a discipline, a means of exploring the world, an aspiration that led eventually to a lifelong career. Words offered me intensity, spectacle, and power.

X. Sparks

A nd what of the bomb atop the schoolyard ring set?
In the explosion's aftermath, Steve and I sat for a long
time in his family's backyard porch swing. Neighbors waited
outside, too, trying to make sense of the massive noise that had
disturbed them. Steve and I eventually heard people going
back into their homes. We lingered outdoors anyway. I worried
that we might start hearing sirens: police cars showing up so
that officers could assess the situation at John J. Cory School;
or, worse yet, an ambulance. The sounds we heard were those
typical of a summer evening: people talking in their yards, kids
laughing or shouting, radios and TVs playing. After a while
Steve and I felt confident enough to go back inside the Fedders'
house.

And during the next few days? I stayed tense, anxious, that
there might be a terrible aftermath. The Fedders received no
visit from police, however, asking what we knew about the
incident; Steve's neighbors dropped no hints nor made snide
comments to Freda and Earl about the noise two or three
nights earlier; and in subsequent days we read no newspaper
accounts beneath the headline "Children Hurt in Mystery
Blast." Does this outcome now seem like an anticlimax? Of
course—but in the best possible way. Up to that moment in
my life I had never experienced such a relief that actions I'd
taken had accomplished *nothing*. For this and other reasons,
Steve and I felt deep relief that although we had disturbed
the peace, our crime had no consequences beyond the sudden
noise, the rattling of windows, and the brief confusion among
the neighbors and their dogs. The bomb turned out to be just
a harmless prank after all. Over the years since then, however,
I've sometimes wakened with a jolt from nightmares in which
someone had been burned, maimed, or blinded as a consequence

of the bomb that Steve and I had designed, engineered, placed, and detonated on that calm summer evening. I still cringe at the recollection that we had set off the explosion without fully grasping the potential consequences. How could we have been so careless? So oblivious to the risks? The outcome could have been far worse. Somehow we just got lucky.[18]

If our mothers and fathers had more fully understood what Steve and I had undertaken during all those years of our pyrotechnic experiments, perhaps Freda, viewing life through a biblical lens, would have quoted Job 5:6-7 as a lament or admonition: "Yet man is born unto trouble, as the sparks fly upward." Maybe so. But Man is born unto insight too, as are Woman, Boy, and Girl. Even causing trouble can lead to insights. Among other things, Steve and I reached insights about the risks we were taking. Our neighbors weren't the only people jolted by the explosion that rattled the windows that night: Steve and I were, too. The summer bomb inoculated us from further pyrotechnic shenanigans. We continued to build fireworks, but only of the more elegant, artistic varieties. As Steve phrased it recently: "We focused on the prettier kinds." Our pyrocopia yielded fountains, pinwheels, cascades, and torches. Rocketry projects proceeded as well but now only in more cautious ways, each more fully thought-through and based on careful designs instead of wild ideas. In short, we kept experimenting, but we did so responsibly.

In addition, we reached other kinds of insights, among them the sparks of understanding that can combine over time into knowledge—flashes of intellectual apprehension, the flare of imagination, the sparkle of intuition, the radiance of friendship. Through this process we expanded our knowledge of the world, of science, of the nature of risk and responsibility. We constructed the foundations that underlay what became our adult careers.[19] We also built a friendship that has now lasted through many life events, including for each of us our respective marriages and our broods of children, and that friendship endures and thrives even as we now approach old age.

One of the consolations of aging can be a deepened clarity about long-past events. (Is this is a consolation prize for the declining faculty of short-term memory?) A recollection surfacing into my awareness now: the Fourth of July in 1964. Steve and I are fourteen years old. We've decided to watch a fireworks display from the Fedders' front yard. I sit with Steve, his parents, and his sister on folding chairs arrayed across the lawn. The slope of the neighborhood and the bowl-like topography of southeast Denver allows us to view the aerials ascending from the University of Denver campus half a mile away. Best of all, we can observe this event with the Rocky Mountains spread out as a backdrop beyond the city. The show begins. Gorgeous aerials blossom in the near-darkness. Then, just a few minutes later, massive thunderheads boil up over the mountains with the abruptness and intensity typical of summer weather in Colorado. The entire western horizon— the vast ridge of the Front Range—flashes with lightning. The Fedders and I can still see the aerials exploding over the DU campus, but, given the thunderstorm beyond, the fireworks now look puny—little zinnias blooming and quickly withering. Freda comments: "Well, God always puts on a better show than we do." I can't disagree with her, though she and I will never reach agreement over who or what God may be. But it's true that the fireworks provide a paltry display compared to the web of miles-long lightning bolts, massive sparks at once terrifying and magnificent, that strike downward onto the foothills and sideways from cloud to cloud. Soon even Steve and I ignore the pyrotechnic display and pay attention only to the thunderstorm.

Afterthoughts

Boxtop Satori

For an American boy growing up in the heartland during the 1950's, the cultural capital of the world wasn't Paris or New York or even Hollywood, but rather Battle Creek, Michigan. And the highest achievement of humankind wasn't art, science, religion, or even baseball—it was the cereal box top premium.

There were three kinds. The first was the least significant: various gliders, rockets, masks, and follow-the-path games printed on a cereal box itself. Most of these premiums scarcely deserved the name. I held them in contempt, though I always tried them out, dissecting each box long before it was empty, or else transferring the contents into another box, a bowl, or the nearest wastebasket.

The second kind of premium offered greater rewards for greater effort. This kind came inside the box. Somewhere down there, nestled safely in Cheerios or Post Toasties or Spoon Size Shredded Wheat, was the object of my longing. All I needed was enough time and appetite to eat my way past the cereal. This was a minor challenge: like most self-respecting boys, I regarded the cereal as little more than packing material for the premium. I usually reached my goal by plunging an arm elbow-deep into the box to settle the matter once and for all. Yet the effort usually proved more exciting than the final achievement. Free-prize-inside premiums tended to be paltry: whistles, balloons, decals, and other affronts to my nascent acquisitiveness.

Then there was the third kind of premium—the kind I mailed away for. This was the best of all possible premiums, though it involved tolerating a typically unreasonable adult request:

PLEASE ALLOW SIX TO EIGHT WEEKS FOR DELIVERY. But
if I sent my money along with a few boxtops, if I remembered
to fill out the order form, if I waited that inexplicably long wait,
then the effort was almost always worthwhile. For in return, I
received a parachute, a crystal radio, a miniature telescope, a
sundial watch, a camera, a first aid kit, a baseball bat-shaped
pencil, a Lone Ranger deputy badge, or any of several strange
rings.

Looking back now, I feel astonished at how desperately I
craved those trinkets, how eagerly I sought them, how quickly
I walked into every marketing snare that the cereal companies
set for me. Was I simply doing my apprenticeship in American
consumerism? I suspect not. Gullibility and greed weren't the
whole story. The truth is that some of those premiums fired my
imagination like few possessions I've owned before or since.

Consider the meteorite ring. The ring itself was unremarkable: just a plastic ring with a clear cap over the top. Inside,
however, was a real meteorite. I could scarcely believe that this
ugly, pitted, gray-brown pebble could have produced one of
the sky-wide streaks of light I loved to spot on summer nights.
I spent a lot of time tilting the ring back and forth, examining
the meteorite, and pondering it. What part of the solar system
was it from? How far had it traveled? How had it survived its
plunge through the atmosphere? Once it fell to Earth, who had
found it? I imagined a special staff clad in white coats and goggles—the General Mills Meteorite Recovery Team—searching
the Nevada desert on hands and knees.

Then there was the atomic ring: the paragon of cereal boxtop
premiums. The atomic ring was a spinthariscope. Consisting of
a sealed tube with a thin layer of radium and other chemicals
at one end and a lens at the other, a spinthariscope is a simple
device for viewing subatomic phenomena. The radium inter-
acts with the other chemicals to produce alpha particles, which
show up as tiny flashes inside the device. (The name comes
from the Greek word spintharis, "spark" + -scope.) The atomic
ring, a version of the basic spinthariscope, was encased in a

mental and plastic ring instead of a larger tube, as would be typical of the devices sometimes present in high school physics classes. This wasn't the likeliest of cereal premiums, but it was definitely the best.

I sent off for mine during the mid-Fifties. I was seven years old. After going to bed each night, I would pull the covers over my head, nestle into the darkness, wait for my eyes to adjust, then peer through the eyepiece and watch what I believed to be the unfolding of a miniature galaxy. Of course I told my family about the ring, but I never convinced anyone of my claims about what I saw there. "I can see shooting stars inside this ring!" I told my parents and brothers. "I can see comets! I can see planets!" Everyone was amused but incredulous. No matter. Knowing that I alone saw the flashes heightened my sense of delight. I had discovered a private universe.

The atomic ring now seems like a bad joke. Just a little more than a decade after the U.S. nuclear attacks on Hiroshima and Nagasaki, a major American food company promoted this radioactive toy, then continued distributing it during the first lap of the US-Soviet nuclear arms race. Yet the atomic ring didn't inspire fear in me. It didn't prompt me to consider the tragedies of World War Two or the quandaries of post-war American military power. When I looked at it, I never saw the engines of Armageddon. I saw a window into another dimension.

I didn't keep any of my old premiums, but even now, many decades after I acquired them, I can still feel their influence. I've graduated from the Secret Agent Microscope and the Lone Ranger Spyglass to more elaborate and subtle technologies, but I would be ungrateful not to acknowledge my original inspiration. I've outgrown my obsession with codes and ciphers, and I can trace some of my fascinations with language to the Secret Code Maker and other premiums. Childhood possessions are notoriously influential. I could have done far worse than to have boxtop premiums sparking my impressionable young mind.

Were the premiums as remarkable as they seemed during my youth? Probably not. Some of them were simply amusing toys. Others were just bits of promotional junk. Yet ultimately their significance, both at the time and since, says less about the trinkets themselves than about human imagination. My own imagination was (and is) a complex force that both animates my psyche and in turn energizes my work as a writer. I owe this aspect of my personality largely to my parents, who were by nature both playful and artistic. However, I owe something as well to the boxtop premiums. It's not as if the premiums were a source of imagination; instead, they were a kind of particle for imagination to grasp, much as water vapor requires a bit of dust to form around before atmospheric moisture can turn to rain. The premiums—whether remarkable, banal, or both—made a difference to me. They allowed me a boyhood testing ground for my sense of wonder.

Whenever I take off the sweater in a dim or dark room, I'm astonished by the intricate swirl of sparks that such a simple action produces. To my eye, it's one of the most beautiful and wondrous of sights. It's as if I'm *inside* a spinthariscope. It's as if I'm chunk of radium flinging off thousands of alpha particles. My hyperactive imagination again? Perhaps.

But wonder is where you find it—even if it first turns up at the bottom of a cereal box.

Notes

"Today a Flying Bear Will Kill Me"

[1] "'Flying Bear' Kills 2 Canadians in Freak Crash," in *Global Post* online, June 9, 2011.

> https://www.pri.org/stories/2011-06-09/flying-bear-kills-2-canadians-freak-crash

"Provincial Gods"

[1] Tyler Bridges, "What Lies Beneath" in *Stanford Magazine* online, January/February 2005. All subsequent quotes and data regarding archaeological research at Chavín, as well as about Chavín's culture, derive from this article.

> http://alumni.stanford.edu/get/page/magazine/article/?article_id=34573

[2] Daniel Engber, "The Human Grease Murders," in *Slate* online, December 17, 2009.

> http://www.slate.com/articles/health_and_science/science/2009/12/the_human_grease_murders.html

See also "The Pishtaco of Peru," in The Not So Innocents Abroad (blog), April 1, 2016.

> http://www.thenotsoinnocentsabroad.com/blog/the-pishtaco-of-peru

"ROTAS-SATOR? SATOR-ROTAS!"

[1] Kile, Jenny. "The Sator Square," in Mysterious Writings: Treasure, Mystery, and Games (online newsletter).

> http://mysteriouswritings.com/the-sator-square/

[2] Unnamed blogger, "The Sator Magic Square," in Taliscope.com (blog).

   http://www.taliscope.com/Sator_en.html

[3] Silver, Sandra Sweeny. "The Sator Square," in Early Church History (blog).

   https://earlychurchhistory.org/christian-symbols/the-roman-rotas-square/

"The Snow Man"

[1] Wallace Stevens, "The Snow Man." *Harmonium*. New York: Alfred P. Knopf, 1923.

"Art of Memory, Art of Forgetting"

[1] "2017 Facts and Figures," The Alzheimers Association. Chicago: The Alzheimers Association, 2018. Citation: pp. 6-7.

[2] Ibid., pp. 18-20.

[3] Borges, Jorge Luis, "Funes the Memorious" in *Labyrinths: Selected Stories and Other Writings*. New York: New Directions Publishing Company, 1962, 1964. Citation: p. 61.

[4] Borges, Jorge Luis, "Funes, His Memory" in *Collected Fictions*. New York: Penguin Books, 1962, 1964. Citation: p. 136.

[5] "People Who Never Forget" in *The Guardian, February 2008*:

   https://www.theguardian.com/science/2017/feb/08/total-recall-the-people-who-never-forget

[6] "Eidetic Memory." Wikipedia:

   https://en.wikipedia.org/wiki/Eidetic_memory

[7] Yates, Frances. *The Art of Memory*. Chicago: University of Chicago Press, 2001. Citation: pp. 26-30.

[8] "Lethe." Wikipedia:

https://en.wikipedia.org/wiki/Lethe

[9] Plato. *The Republic*. New York: Penguin Classics, 2007.

"Don't Jump!"

[1] "Asteroid Survey: NASA says 4,700 Space Rocks 'Possibly Hazardous'" in HuffingtonPost.com, December 6, 2017.

https://www.huffingtonpost.com/2012/05/16/asteroid-survey-4700-possibly- hazardous-nasa_n_1522762.html

[2] Elizabeth Kolbert, "2004: Greenland" in *Lapham's Quarterly*, IX-2 (Spring 2016), page 25.

[3] Elizabeth Kolbert, biographical note, *Lapham's Quarterly*, IX-2 (Spring 2016), page 9.

[4] The Heartland Institute online:

https://www.heartland.org/Center-Climate-Environment/index.html

[5] Naomi Klein, *This Changes Everything* (New York: Simon & Schuster, 2014), p.45.

[6] Ibid., p. 45.

[7] Ibid., p. 46.

[8] Naomi Oreskes, "Exxon's Climate Concealment" in *The New York Times* online, October 9, 2015.

http://www.nytimes.com/2015/10/10/opinion/exxons-climate-concealment.html?_r=0

[9] Ibid.

[10] Ibid.

[11] Michael Slezak, "New Study Confirms the Oceans Are Warming Rapidly" in *TheGuardian*.com, June 26, 2017.

https://www.theguardian.com/environment/climate-consensus-97-per-cent/2017/jun/26/new-study-confirms-the-oceans-are-warming-rapidly

[12] Oliver Sacks, quoted by Peter Selgin, "Swimming with Oliver," *Colorado Review*, Vol. 43, No. 1, Spring 2016.

[13] "Germanwings Crash: What Happened in the Final 30 Minutes" in BBC News online, March 23, 2017.

> https://www.bbc.com/news/world-europe-32072218

"Deja, Presque, Jamais Vu"

1 Joseph Heller, *Catch-22* (New York: Simon & Schuster, 1961), p. 214.

[citation?]

> https://www.comparativereligion.com/reincarnation.html

[2] "25% of Americans Believe in Reincarnation" in *Tricycle*, August 10, 2010.

> https://tricycle.org/trikedaily/25-americans-believe-reincarnation/

[3] Ernest Valea, "Reincarnation: Its Meaning and Consequences—Part A: Reincarnation in World Religions," in ComparativeReligion.com.

[4] Ernest Valea, "Reincarnation: Its Meaning and Consequences—Part D: Reincarnation in Modern Thinking," in ComparativeReligion. com.

> https://www.comparativereligion.com/reincarnation.html

[5] Alex Lickerman, M.D., "The Problem with Reincarnation," in *Psychology Today*, October 14, 2012.

> https://www.psychologytoday.com/us/blog/happiness-in-world/201210/the-problem-reincarnation

[6] Tom Schroder, "Ian Stevenson: Sought to Document Memories of Past Lives in Children," in *The Washington Post*, February 11, 2007.

[7] "Ian Stevenson," in Wikipedia. https://en.wikipedia.org/wiki/Ian_Stevenson

[8] Schroder, op. cit.

[9] Ken McLeod, "Reflections on Dzongsar Khyentse's 'How We Raise Tulkus,'" in *Tricycle*, September 15, 2015.

https://tricycle.org/trikedaily/reflections-on-dzongsar-khyentses-how-we-raise-tulkus/

[10] "The Tibetan Tradition of Recognizing Reincarnate Lamas," in Shambhala.com.

https://www.shambhala.com/snowlion_articles/the-tibetan-tradition-of-recognizing-reincarnate-lamas/

[11] Ramin Etesemai, The Tulku System in Tibetan Buddhism: Its Reliability, Orthodoxy and Social Impacts. Unpublished dissertation.

http://research.thanhsiang.org/sites/default/files/attachment/5.%20The%20Tulku%20System%20in%20Tibetan%20Buddhism%20by%20Ramin%20Etesami.pdf

[12] "Past Life Regression" in Wikipedia.

https://en.wikipedia.org/wiki/Past_life_regression

[13] Ann C. Barham, *The Past Life Perspective: Discovering Your True Nature Across Multiple Lifetimes* (New York: Atria/Enliven Books, 2016), pp. 12-13.

[14] "Past Life Regression" on Betty Moore-Hafter's site CreativeEFT.com.

https://creativeeft.com/past-life-regression-2/

[15] "Past Life Regression," in The Skeptic's Dictionary [online].

http://skepdic.com/pastlife.html

[16] "Past Life Regression," Moore-Hafter, op. cit.

https://creativeeft.com/past-life-regression-2/

[17] "Past-Life Regression" in The APA [American Psychological Association] *Dictionary of Psychology* online.

https://dictionary.apa.org/past-life-regression

[18] Harriet Hall, "Past-Life Regression Therapy: Encouraging Fantasy," in Science-Based Medicine online.

https://sciencebasedmedicine.org/past-life-regression-therapy-encouraging-fantasy/

[19] "Hypnotic Regression to Previous Lives," in "Concerns about Hypnotic Regression" in Division of Perceptual Studies / University of Virginia School of Medicine online.

https://med.virginia.edu/perceptual-studies/resources/concerns-about-hypnotic-regression/

[20] "Battle of Messines," in Wikipedia.

https://en.wikipedia.org/wiki/Battle_of_Messines_(1917)

The Allies' detonation deep under German positions was so massive that its shock wave was audible "as far away as London and Dublin":

The 1917 Messines mines detonation was probably the largest planned explosion in history prior to the Trinity atomic weapon test in July 1945 and the largest non-nuclear planned explosion before the British explosive efforts on the Heligoland Islands in April 1947. The Messines detonation is history's deadliest non-nuclear man-made explosion. Several of the mines at Messines did not go off on time. On 17 July 1955, lightning set one off, killing a cow. Another mine, which had been abandoned as a result of its discovery by German counter-miners, is believed to have been found but no attempt has been made to remove it.

[21] The Commonwealth War Graves Commission online.

https://www.cwgc.org

[22] "Past Life Regression" in Wikipedia.

https://en.wikipedia.org/wiki/Past_life_regression

[23] "Past Life Regression," in The Skeptic's Dictionary online.

http://skepdic.com/pastlife.html

[24] Gilbert Murray, *Five Stages of Greek Religion* (London: Watts & Col, 1935, 1946), p. 171.

"9/14"

[1] "2001 Anthrax Attacks" in Wikipedia.

> https://en.wikipedia.org/wiki/2001_anthrax_attacks

[2] "American Airlines Flight 587" in Wikipedia.

> https://en.wikipedia.org/wiki/American_Airlines_Flight_587

"Pyrocopia"

[1] Spitz, R.A. *The First Year of Life : A Psychoanalytic Study of Normal and Deviant Development of Object Relations.* New York, 1965: International Universities Press.

[2] Bowlby, John. *Attachment. Attachment and Loss,* vol. 1, 2nd ed. New York: Basic Books, 1969, 1999.

[3] —. *Separation: Anxiety & Anger. Attachment and Loss,* vol. 2. London: Hogarth Press, 1973.

[4] —. *Loss: Sadness & Depression. Attachment and Loss,* vol. 3. London: Hogarth Press, 1980.

[5] —. *A Secure Base: Parent-Child Attachment and Healthy Human Development.* London: Routledge, 1988.

[6] No correspondence or other written records survive in which my parents describe to friends or relatives what took place within the family at that time. However, a 30 November 1964 letter to my father from Erwin R. Goodenough, a professor of religious studies at Yale and Brandeis universities, responds to whatever my dad had sent Goodenough some weeks earlier regarding Rick's removal from the family. "Your letter is really moving," Goodenough states. "When I reached the part in which you said you had had to choose between Estela [my mother] and Rick, and tell him to his face that all family ties were cut off, I could hardly take it. My God, what it must have meant to you! After your years and years of struggling to save him." Goodenough also comments on "the apparent steadiness of the other boys" and "the fantastic strength which seems never to fail you."

[7] While it's true that many of the local boys I knew could be obnoxious, I severely overreacted in considering them juvenile delinquents and labeling them "hoodlums." Most were harmless. I realized decades later that the boys I found abrasive, competitive, derisive, and sometimes hostile during our boyhood were simply immature. I was stunned to discover in recent years that most of them eventually outgrew their annoying attributes, matured, and became productive, even creative members of society. By exploring social media sites, I learned that Jimmy Brink, whom I had once branded a "hood," had become a teacher and, later, the esteemed headmaster of a private academy in Los Angeles. Jim Lysaght, another boy I found dismissive and sometimes hostile, became a well-regarded photographer for both *The Denver Post* and *The Rocky Mountain News.* Randy Zimmerman served in the Navy for ten years, then worked for the rest of his life as an aviation mechanic. Bruce Hurd taught school throughout adulthood until his death in 2007. In short, these boys were boyish during boyhood; then they grew up into responsible, productive men. The process was no different for me. (The mother of a childhood friend once told me bluntly when I visited her decades later, during my fifties: "At that same age, you were no picnic, either.")

[8] Among other projects, Steve and I even cooked up our own spy agency, CIPHER by name. This effort took shape during the heyday of James Bond movies, as well as TV shows like The Man from U.N.C.L.E. and Secret Agent. The acronym CIPHER stood for Conspiracy for Intelligence, Panic, Havoc, Espionage, and Revenge. Our mission? That was never entirely clear. Our equipment consisted of home-made gadgets, miniature flashlights, secret inks, and a variety ineffective tools designed for picking locks. A "big ear"-like eavesdropping device never came to fruition. Our activities included skulking around in the neighborhood, climbing walls at the elementary and junior high schools, and observing neighbors for no clear reason but without intent to do further mischief. At some point my father gently noted that "cipher" means "nothing": "It's essentially it's a synonym for zero," he told me. "For emptiness."

[9] There is ongoing controversy about the nature of boys' friendships compared to girls'. Even a cursory review of the literature on this topic

reveals multiple and often conflicting assumptions. Judy Y. Chu's article "Adolescent Boys' Friend-ships and Peer Group Culture" provides a thoughtful overview of the discussions and contradictions within the social-science literature. "Developmental research on adolescent friendships has consistently shown boys to have fewer close friendships and to experience lower levels of intimacy within these relationships as compared with girls," Chu writes. But she adds that, "This literature . . . neglects to account for boys who develop close, same-sex friendships despite obstacles presented by their peer group culture and how these boys draw strength from their close friendships to resist social pressures that might otherwise constrain their behaviors and self-expression." Lamentably, social scientists often draw conclusions that are full of empirical confidence but that ignore the variety, complexity, and sometimes paradoxical aspects of actual human beings' lives. (See Judy Y. Chu, "Adolescent Boys' Friendships and Peer Group Culture" in *New Directions for Child and Adolescent Development*, no. 107, Spring 2005.)

[10] Other male friends, both during early adolescence and later, included Scott T. and Palle Y. Scott shared my interest in rocketry and the sciences, though we didn't collaborate as closely as Steve and I did on building models. Scott and I also became hiking buddies: we ventured frequently into the Rockies during our late teens and traveled to Peru during our twenties, where we explored ancient ruins and trekked throughout the north-central Peruvian Andes. Palle, the son of European academics, became a close friend for many years, with the nature of our friendship emphasizing music, literature, and other arts. Starting at around age twelve, I also started focusing my attention on female peers. Close friends and early girlfriends included Mindy J., who shared my interests in the arts and in outdoor sports; and Anita D., a gifted writer who became my first peer-mentor on literary efforts.

[11] Steve and I found *Ideal Marriage* hilarious in many ways. This book was, after all, forty years out of date by the time we discovered it. Among other critics, feminist writers of the 1960's and 70's derided van de Velde's book as sanctimonious and condescending toward women. (One writer described it as "the perfect manual for couples

who prefer their sex accompanied by the hosannahs of angels.") A typical passage:

> In any erotic play executed with delicate reverence and consideration—and, above all, when the lovers have not become quite accustomed and attuned to one another—a considerable amount of time should be given to kisses and manual caresses before the genitals are touched. . . . Only by a cautious and circuitous route should [the hands] approach the holy place of sex and tenderly seek admittance.

Nevertheless, *Ideal Marriage* was certainly far more informative, as well as much more respectful of women, than was true for the locker-room banter and the men's-magazine articles that provided mid-century American boys with most of their information about sex. The book was also a better source compared to the offensive sex-education lectures that Steve and I and our male peers had to endure from Dr. Zarlengo, the misogynistic, homophobic, derisive, profane medical director for the Denver Public Schools at that time.

> https://en.wikipedia.org/wiki/Ideal_Marriage:_Its_Physiology_and_Technique

[12] In his marvelous memoir *Uncle Tungsten,* the physician-author Oliver Sacks, who was obsessed with chemistry from boyhood on, laments the trend toward obsessive safety. "Now, of course, none of these [dangerous] chemicals can be bought, and even school or museum laboratories are increasingly confined to reagents that are less hazardous—and less fun." Sacks goes on to quote the American chemist Linus Pauling's lament on this same issue:

> Just think of the differences today. A young person gets interested in chemistry and is given a chemistry set. But it doesn't contain potassium cyanide. It doesn't even contain copper sulfate or anything else interesting because all the interesting chemicals are considered dangerous substances. Therefore, these budding young chemists don't have a chance to do anything engrossing with their chemistry sets.

[Sacks, Oliver. *Uncle Tungsten*. New York: Vintage, 2002. Citation: p. 86, footnote.]

That said, there's no question that some children and teenagers used chemistry sets in dangerous ways. Even supervised classroom activities could lead to hazardous situations that wouldn't be tolerated today. In our eighth- or ninth-grade biology class, Steve and I survived a mishap in which a fellow-student inadvertently left an open container of ether on a horizontal ventilation duct, dispersing the anesthetic throughout the room and sickening all the students present. I'm also astonished when I recall that science teachers allowed us to examine and even play with large beads of mercury.

[13] "Catalog #631." Penrose, Colo.: Estes Industries, Inc., 1963, p. 1.

[14] Daniel Ellsberg, writing in *The Doomsday Machine: Confessions of a Nuclear War Planner* (New York and London: Bloomsbury, 2017), states that U.S. strategy during the late 1950's and early 1960's focused on an all-out response in the event of U.S.-Soviet nuclear war. Pentagon officials at the time estimated that this approach would lead to a worldwide death toll of approximately 600 million people within the first weeks after a nuclear exchange. Ellsberg considers these estimates to be low; a better guess would be at least a billion fatalities. Even these estimates didn't consider subsequent deaths likely from famine, illness, the delayed consequences of radiation poisoning, and "nuclear winter." Ellsberg assumes that many more hundreds of millions of fatalities would have resulted during that era. The world's human population in 1962 was 3.5 billion people. Half, two thirds, or even a greater proportion of humanity might have died in a 1960's-era nuclear war.

[15] Robert Jay Lifton, M.D., a psychiatrist who taught at the Yale University School of Medicine for many decades, has commented eloquently about how people sometimes express their anxieties and fears about nuclear war by identifying with rather than by rejecting the weapons that put all of us—and, indeed, all life on Earth—at risk. Dr. Lifton has noted that, among other things, American culture has absorbed many nuclear terms, phrases, and images into common parlance in ways that renders terrifying issues relatively harmless. This process of absorbtion has made it possible for many people to

live out the subtitle of Stanley Kubrick's Cold War-era movie, *Dr. Strangelove; or, How I Learned to Stop Worrying and Love the Bomb.* When I interviewed Dr. Lifton many years ago regarding nuclear imagery and nuclear obsessions, he told me, "Now it seems that many people are identifying with the Bomb and its power in certain ways. There's a fascination with [its] death-dealing power. Consider the *[Dr.] Strangelove* phenomenon. At the end of the movie, one of the characters ride a bomb out of the plane toward its target, and he gives out a big yell. It's a mixture of a desparate anti-nuclear cry and a kind of nuclear 'high.'" Quoted from Edward Myers, *The Chosen Few: Surviving the Nuclear Holocaust.* South Bend, Indiana: And Books, 1982. Citation: page 170.

[16] George Plimpton, *Fireworks: A History and Celebration.* New York: Doubleday & Company, 1984, page 9.

[17] Sacks, *Uncle Tungsten*, p. 87.

[18] Another incident in which Steve and I got lucky took place during 1967, when we were both seventeen. At this stage of our lives, mountaineering had replaced pyrotechnics as our chief shared interest. We had been avid hikers for many years. Our fathers had often chauffeured us up to the mountains for warm-weather excursions throughout our early and mid-teens. Once we reached driving age at sixteen, however, Steve and I could drive ourselves. This new degree of freedom led to more frequent, more ambitious, and often more dangerous ventures in the Rockies.

At some point during the summer of 1967, we made one of our routine ascents of Mt. Bierstadt, altitude 14,065 feet. Mt. Bierstadt isn't a technically challenging peak; it's basically just a huge pile of granite boulders. But therein lay the temptation, the risk, and the potential disaster that Steve and I put into play. Just a few hundred feet below the summit, we noticed a massive rock, probably four feet wide and five feet tall, balanced on a tiny pedestal. We had watched enough Roadrunner cartoons to know that if you gave this kind of boulder even a modest shove, it would tip over and fall into the valley. Or not. Maybe that happened only in cartoons. What were the odds, really, that we could replicate Wile E. Coyote's iconic maneuver? Surely the two of us couldn't topple a one-ton chunk of granite! We scanned the landscpe to make sure that no other hikers were coming up the slope. Then, without further reconnaisance or discussion, we shoved the rock. It tipped, fell forward with dreamlike slowness, started downward, and, taking other rocks with it, began its inexorable descent.

Once again Steve and I realized that we had set something literally in motion that couldn't be recalled. We looked out again over the panorama below Mt. Bierstadt. Was it possible that other hikers might be down there after all? Was it possible that such a huge boulder might roll down the mountain but then simply keep rolling—might descend from the peak but then angle to the right, follow the valley's curvature, and proceed until it entered the inhabited areas above Georgetown? Might it not crash into, or through, one or more of the cabins there? Once again we had a belated realization that certain actions taken can't be taken; certain deeds can't be undone. We watched closely as the boulder tumbled all the way down Mt. Bierstadt, a vertical drop of at least 3,000 feet and a transit of almost a mile. Then, without warning, the massive rock smashed into a granite abutment and came to an abupt halt.

That was the last time Steve and I ever pushed a rock off a cliff. While this incident failed to win us the 1968 Nobel Prize for Adolescent Male Stupidity, I suspect that the committee members in Oslo gave us careful consideration before moving on (perhaps reluctantly) to select some other teenager for that year's award.

[19] In our conversations over the years, Steve has been modest about his youthful knowledge of chemistry. As he wrote to me in a recent e-mail: "Near as I can recall, I had no real chemistry knowledge at the time we ordered the cookbook; I think we fiddled with the recipes some, but based on performance of powder blends rather than applying any chemistry principles. In fact, even a chemistry major college graduate wouldn't have much insight beyond the need for an oxidizer and reducer and an appreciation for how the addition of other salts produces color." Whether his modesty is appropriate or not, Steve certainly understood much more about chemistry than I did at the time; and I find it difficult to believe that the enjoyable process we shared in designing, building, and igniting fireworks didn't somehow feed into his more serious studies of chemistry from high school through college and into his decades-long career.

Acknowledgments

AS IS ALWAYS TRUE, I owe deep gratitude to Edith, Robin, and Cory for their support, patience, and encouragement. In addition, I want to thank the following people for their assistance of specific kinds (or many kinds) as I wrote some of these essays:

Jim Barszcz
Deborah Black, M.D.
David Cain
Caroline Dumaine
Steve Fedder and Patty McBride
Betty Moore-Hafter
Burt Kimmelman and Diane Simmons
Andy Sweet and Nancy Rainwater
John Silbersack
Scott Thomas
Laurance Thompson
Meredith Sue Willis

About the Author

BORN IN DENVER and raised in Colorado, Mexico, and Peru, E. J. Myers attended Grinnell College and the University of Denver. He has worked in a wide variety of professions and trades, including inpatient health care, emergency medical services, carpentry, cabinetmaking, and publishing. He is the author of forty-two published books, most issued by mainstream companies, among them four novels (*The Mountain Made of Light, Fire and Ice, The Summit,* and *Last Things*); fourteen children's books; and a well-received, much-reprinted book about bereavement, *When Parents Die: A Guide for Adults.* He has also co-authored or ghostwritten over a dozen books for clients or other authors. He lives with his wife in central Vermont.

For information about E. J. Myers, visit his Web site at:

www.edwardmyerswriter.net

About Montemayor Press

MONTEMAYOR PRESS is an independent publisher of literature for adults and children. To learn more about our books, visit:

www.MontemayorPress.com

or write for a catalogue at:

Montemayor Press
P. O. Box 546
Montpelier, VT 05601

Books by E. J. Myers
Available from
Montemayor Press

Fiction

Mission - 978-1-932727-34-7
Fever - 978-1-932727-17-3
Last Things - 978-1-932727-24-1

The Mountain Trilogy

The Mountain Made of Light - 978-1-932727-04-3
Fire and Ice - 978-1-932727-06-7
The Summit - 978-1-932727-07-3

Nonfiction

On Whitcomb Hill - 978-1-932727-32-6
Lovely, Dark and Deep - 978-1-932727-26-5
Pond Meadow Moon - 978-1-932727-29-6
The Whiteness of the Weasel - 978-1-932727-31-9

Books for Children

The Adventures of Forri the Baker - 978-0-9674477-0-4
Climb or Die - 978-1-932727-12-8
Duck and Cover - 978-0-9674477-8-X
Ice - 978-0-9674477-9-8
Solos en la Montaña - 978-1-932727-18-0
Survival of the Fittest - 978-0-9674477-2-8

www.ingramcontent.com/pod-product-compliance
Lightning Source LLC
Chambersburg PA
CBHW070928260626
47162CB00007B/2833